WHAT'S UNDER YOUR CAPE?

Barbara Gruener

SUPERHEROES OF THE CHARACTER KIND

Keep on crusading for GOOD!! :)

Cape UP,
Barbara

FERNE PRESS

Summary: A guide to help elementary teachers infuse virtues, values, and traits into the habits, routines, and culture of their character-building so that their superheroes can soar.

Library of Congress Cataloging-in-Publication Data
Gruener, Barbara
What's Under Your Cape? SUPERHEROES of the Character Kind/Barbara Gruener-
First Edition
ISBN-13: 978-1-938326-33-2
1. Character education. 2. Elementary students. 3. Teachers. 4. Character traits.
I. Gruener, Barbara II. Title
Library of Congress Control Number: 2014938605

FERNE PRESS

Ferne Press is an imprint of Nelson Publishing & Marketing
366 Welch Road, Northville, MI 48167
www.nelsonpublishingandmarketing.com
(248) 735-0418

Dedication

To my beautiful extended family—Mom and Harold, Dad and Flo, Bobby and Ruby, Clay and Sue, David and Cynthia, and my siblings—and to my kindhearted husband, John, and our precious children, Kaitlyn, Jacob, and Joshua. I'm grateful every day for all of you, and I am blessed by your continued support and unconditional love.

Acknowledgments

If this book plants a few seeds that'll grow and bear fruit in your classroom character-building, it's because of the many superheroes in my life who have helped make this dream a reality. I thank my parents for the life lessons that I learned on my family farm. I also owe a debt of gratitude to all of my teachers along the way, from my 4-H leaders to my K–12 teachers, to my college professors at the University of Wisconsin-Madison, and to the faculty at the University of Houston-Clear Lake. Teachers are miracle workers, and they all played an integral part in shaping who I've become.

I appreciate and thank my wonderful community and school family in Friendswood ISD and specifically at Westwood-Bales. Thank you for being open to my ideas and suggestions, even when they seemed over-the-top or outlandish.

To my mentor, Sally Roher; what an honor it was to learn and grow under your guidance. Your support and encouragement kept me going when my learning curve was steep and I wasn't sure I could persevere. I miss you so much and every day I strive to be like you.

To my friends at the Josephson Institute of Ethics and at the Character Education Partnership; thank you for the training and opportunities I've experienced through our partnership. In fact, it was at CEP's 20th National Forum in Washington, DC, where I met my publisher, Marian Nelson. I was instantly inspired by Marian's passion and verve for children and life and I'm so blessed that she believed in me and in this project.

Thank you to Kris Yankee, my sharp and diligent editor, for her patience, time, and talent. What a pleasure to work with such a caring professional.

I thank my close friends who are always there for me to share my blessings and my burdens: Audrey, Carol, Debra, Jane Ann, Jennifer, Kim, Laura, and Lisa.

Finally, thank you to my husband and children. My life is better because of you.

Contents

Introduction

Growing up on a large dairy farm in Wisconsin, I didn't get to watch much, if any, television. Oh, we did see an occasional episode of *The Waltons, Marcus Welby, M.D.*, and *Eight Is Enough*. But I'll always remember the kids at school talking about shows like *Gilligan's Island* and the time(s) the shipwrecked crew was almost rescued. It was then that I wished my life included more fantasy. We didn't have time for comic books, either, so I didn't even know anything about Batman, Spiderman, or Aquaman until I was older. My superheroes were my parents, the pastor at our church, my teachers, and my 4-H leader.

From the day I was old enough to join, I was a member of our local 4-H Chapter. It was so much fun because we had monthly social time at our meetings, periodic gatherings like skating parties, events like our June Dairy Month Celebration (oh, how I loved giving away cheese and crackers at the banks and local grocery stores!), and an annual opportunity to showcase what we'd learned at the County Fair. There we competed against other 4-H students in categories like sewing, baking, gardening, and animals. We showed our blue-ribbon registered Holstein cows and calves. Each summer, we'd load the animals into a trailer and drive thirty minutes down the road to the fairgrounds in DePere, where they'd stay for a week on display for fair-goers to view and judges to judge. That County Fair was a much-anticipated event that wouldn't have happened had we not been in 4-H. I love what 4-H stands for and the pledge explains it really well:

"I pledge my head to clearer thinking, my heart to greater loyalty, my hands to larger service, and my health to better living, for my club, my community, my country, and my world."

Actually, the words "and my world" were added after I'd been a member for a while, and I vividly remember how hard it was to adjust to that new phrase being a part of something I held dear. Head. Heart. Hands. Health. All tools that heroes use. All parts of a whole. All important individually and incredibly powerful collectively. And, all domains of character development.

Children aren't born with good character; it develops over time. But they are hard-wired to learn, and their capacity for character is unlimited. At Westwood-Bales Elementary, a State and National School of Character, we start to introduce our virtues when we get our littlest learners at four years of age.

I pledge my head to clearer thinking... . The first domain of character development is the cognitive domain. Just like in the 4-H pledge, it starts with the head. We must teach the values that we want woven into the DNA of our students' lives through direct instruction, indirect modeling, and daily reinforcement. We must show them the behaviors that go along with the value words so that they can know what the words look like in terms of how they act. We are making cognitive connections to character at every turn. Students must be cognizant of what the word "respect," for example, looks like, sounds like, and feels like, and then how it connects to them and how they treat one another. We teach it proactively so that it becomes an action verb that they can understand, appreciate, and embrace.

I pledge my heart to greater loyalty... . Once our superheroes know the values, what they mean, and how they connect, the character road takes us to the affective domain, the heart. We'll move from knowing the virtues to embracing them, to loving what they stand for and how they feel. Our chances of students using the virtues as their moral compass increase dramatically when they love the values, when they've made room for them in their heart, and when they've let them become a part of who they are, what they want to be, and how they act. A huge part of helping students embrace the values is giving them a voice and encouraging them to express how foundational traits like integrity, fairness, kindness, and empathy add value to their lives.

I pledge my hands to larger service… . From the affective domain, we travel to the behavioral arena. Once a child knows the virtues and feels and embraces them, it's time for action. Principle 5 of the Character Education Partnership's *The 11 Principles of Effective Character Education* puts it this way: "We must provide opportunities for moral action…students are constructive learners—they learn best by doing."[1] We must put character in their hands and then turn it over to them. When we step out of the role of teacher and into the role of cheerleader and coach, students can forge ahead with their ideas and their passion to make things better for their world. Ask them; they'll know what they want to do. Once they've entered the behavioral domain, all they'll need is a little guidance and a ride. You will be pleasantly surprised at the big difference little ones can make if the adults in their lives move over a bit and get out of their way.

I pledge my health to better living… . Our chance to put it all together is encompassed by the ethical domain, or from the 4-H pledge, our health. Every day we each wake up with a choice. We can help or we can hurt. We can lift people up or tear them down. We can make things better or make them worse. It's all about choices. But remember, we aren't born with good character, so these good choices won't happen because we want or expect them to; they also won't be made in isolation. The Ashanti proverb, "It takes a village to raise a child"[2] certainly rings true. We have to intentionally flood their world with character talk, character love, and opportunities for character action. We can't leave anything to chance. If we want our superheroes to use those powers for good, we must harness that ethical energy into our character force field. Character kids will lead healthier, happier lives, satisfied knowing that the world is better because of them, their values, and their choices.

But how do we cover all of those domains and still find time to teach the academic content that our twenty-first-century learners need to succeed? It was Helen Keller who said, "Character cannot be developed in ease and quiet. Only through experience of trial and suffering can the soul be strengthened, ambition inspired, and success achieved."[3]

My suggestion throughout this guidebook will be to seize teachable moments throughout your day to infuse character development opportunities and lessons into your daily content and curriculum. The modes by which I often encourage doing this are through chants and songs to seal the deal, through meaningful movement to spark brain activity, and with laughter and positivity in a climate where students feel safe and secure.

Why sing? We can't all talk at the same time, but we can all sing at the same time. In harmony even. Talk about your unifying activity. How did you remember your ABCs? Probably by learning and singing the "Alphabet Song." When I taught high school Spanish, my first lesson was singing the Spanish alphabet with those teenagers. And guess what? More times than not, they'd come to the oral quiz asking if they could sing it instead of recite it. Yep, sealing the deal with a song is a promising practice.

Why dance? In his book *Brain Rules: 12 Principles for Surviving and Thriving at Work, Home, and School,* Dr. John Medina discusses the benefit of meaningful movement on the brain. He refers to physical activity as "cognitive candy." In fact, the brain's chemistry thrives on movement. Professor Medina says that exercise can actually trigger the tiny proteins known as brain-derived neurotrophic factor (BDNF) and act "like Miracle-Gro® for the brain."[4] He advocates giving students a brain break every ten minutes, all day long. Just imagine how cognitively refreshing that would be.

Why laugh? A popular maxim tells us, "Laughter is the best medicine." But how is that possible? Laughter sparks chemicals in the body that have been proven to reduce stress and strengthen our immune systems. It can also boost energy and diminish pain. If we can give our students permission to be funny and to laugh, we'll be able to capitalize on those natural highs and medicinal benefits that come from laughter.

It was in the movie *Field of Dreams* when Kevin Costner's character coined the phrase "If you build it, they will come." In my thirty years of experience in schools, whether in a pre-K classroom or working with high school seniors, students are more likely to engage and connect with content when it's authentic, creative, moving, and fun.

Focus on your students' strengths and superpowers, and then watch how they develop. Thank you for your interest in my strategies for success with your superheroes.

Chapter 1

S IS FOR SERVICE

Superheroes are all about service. The scene goes like this: The villain is threatening to take over the town and the superhero sees the need and jumps into action. Service with a smile, problem solved, and the day is saved. Superheroes have a strong moral code and simply cannot help but fly to the rescue and serve. And to those naysayers who think that children need to be a certain age to serve, I say, "Holy cow, Batman!"

As a farmer's daughter, I was working in the barn at the ripe old age of two. I owned my first calf and was helping with chores by the time I went off to kindergarten. We milked about fifty cows until the time of my tenth birthday, when we built a milking parlor and increased our herd size to 250. Every morning before school and every afternoon after, duty called and I put on my barn clothes to milk those cows, sixteen at a time. Not only did I learn responsibility, work ethic, and service at a very young age, but I also practiced them day in and day out until these values became my superpowers.

When I left my family farm for college and beyond, I was well-equipped to take my place in the world, to show up on time, to work hard, and to serve with a smile. Service creates a win-win because the helper feels needed while filling needs.

At schools of character, every student serves, whether it's something seemingly small, like being the line leader or caboose, or a little more involved like serving on safety patrol. Every job is important and valued because every job meets a need. Some task ideas that might give superheroes the opportunity to serve include:

★ Morning Leader: This student leads the pledges (at our school, we say the Pledge of Allegiance, Texas pledge, and character pledge) and announces birthdays each morning in the community gathering.

★ Door Holder: This child holds the door open while the class is coming and going.

★ Watt Watcher: This child is in charge of turning out the lights when the class has left the room.

★ Weather Forecaster: This student is in charge of checking the weather forecast and sharing it with the students.

★ Technical Engineer: This student runs the technology for the day.

★ Pencil Sharpener: This child is in charge of keeping the pencils sharpened.

★ Service Patrol: These students help with breakfast in the cafeteria and with car and bus arrival procedures.

★ Green Team: These students serve in the nature center.

★ Recycling Team: These students collect the recycling from bins in every classroom at the end of every week.

★ Bathroom Brigade: These students check the cleanliness of the bathrooms to report any issues and give a weekly report.

★ Paparazzi: This student is in charge of the character camera so that we have pictures to post on the school website.

SERVICE-LEARNING PROJECTS

The natural next step is to turn these service opportunities into service-learning projects. According to the National Service Learning Clearinghouse, "Service-learning is a teaching and learning strategy that integrates meaningful community service with instruction and reflection to enrich the learning experience, teach civic responsibility, and strengthen communities."[5]

While I was searching for exactly that ten years ago, I heard a parent mention that her daughter had started knitting and had really taken to the craft. That sparked the idea that has snowballed into an amazingly fruitful effort for our school and allows for partnership with the community at large. The Knit-For-Service Club began in 2004 with twenty members and has grown to eighty-plus boys and girls who knit to help others. The first year, we made one patchwork blanket to donate to Harold, the King of the Valentine's Day Dance, at his retirement home. Since then, we have collectively knit over two dozen blankets and two thousand baby hats for people in need. The second year, we invited those inaugural club members to keep up their skills by coming back as mentors to the rookie knitters.

In our third year, Save the Children® in Connecticut asked us to join its *Caps to the Capital* campaign. That visit resulted in our club's effort to rally the community to help us send 329 handmade caps to developing countries to help reduce the infant mortality rate. Consequently, we were invited that January to deliver a basket of those caps to the White House. Elizabeth, our young Westwood Ambassador, left one of her hats with the First Lady's chief of staff. When asked how it felt to leave her handiwork with the First Lady, Elizabeth remarked, "It was okay, I suppose. But I really made that hat for a baby." A project with a purpose. Be still my beating heart.

The following year and one hundred knitters strong, our club made preemie-sized hats to donate locally and four afghans, two of which were adult-sized blankets in rival Texas college colors that were auctioned off at our school's spring carnival. The other two were baby-sized throws to give to The Center for Pregnancy locally for an expectant mom. That August, *Highlights* magazine shared the story nationally in the "Gallant Kids" column.[6]

Two years later, when Save the Children® once again called for caps in their Knit One, Save One initiative, the Westwood knitters donated an amazing 652 caps, many made by the children themselves, others made by community stakeholders whom we rallied, including grandmothers, shut-ins, and random friends who read about us in the newspaper or saw us on television or the Internet. We were represented one more time at the Capitol when Hannah, that year's Westwood Ambassador, headed to DC with the club's new leader after I turned the reins over and joined the ranks of volunteers.

A few of our stakeholders include Herman, who donated his wife's supply of yarn after her passing so that our children could put it to good use, and the local knitting guild, which sends volunteers to help just because they want to serve. And Frank, who sends us the yarn he collects from his bi-annual church garage sale in Illinois, and Grace, who suffers from emphysema but knits for us from her oxygen tent. Then there's eight-year-old Makenna, who traveled to the nation's capital to meet with President Obama's staff and to Capitol Hill to lobby for a cause so that her voice could be heard as she exercised her civic rights. And the babies whose lives we've saved and their moms, dads, and siblings who are forever grateful. Students research the places where we could send our hats or blankets, learn to knit, which includes some poetry and patterns, math and fine motor skills, and reflect on how they've made a difference with journal entries or letters. When we partner with Save the Children®, there is a letter-writing component. Each hat is sent with a letter to the president asking for his help to reduce infant mortality. We also attach a note to the families on each cap that we make. During the years when Save the Children® isn't accepting hats, we send them overseas with missionaries or to local hospitals.

When a picture comes back from the field of one of our hats warming the head of a baby in Ethiopia, Malawi, or Bangladesh, we're sure that this intergenerational service-learning opportunity, which started simply within our school walls, has generated a synergy that has touched our community and rippled out to positively impact our world. Superheroes have the power to save lives.

Other service opportunities that we've successfully completed over the years include:

The Undy 500: We collected underwear for orphaned children in Ukraine. As they brought in undies, children wrote their names on a paper pair of boxers so that we could track our donations. Posted on the walls, these papers circled the school as a visual reminder of how we were helping the whole human race. The project culminated in a school-wide assembly on the track outside circling our donations, which were placed out on the field spelling out "U-500" so that we could get an aerial photo. But how would we pay to ship the 3,479 pairs of underwear that were donated? I asked that very question to a class of third graders and one knew exactly what we could do when she emphatically exclaimed, "We could ask Dr. Phil. He helps people all of the time!"

At her suggestion, I reached out to Dr. Phil McGraw. Sadly, I did not get a response. When I was in Washington, DC, that fall, I was telling the story to the other Dr. Phil, Phil Vincent from the Character Development Group. He asked how much money I thought it would take to ship all of those undies to Ukraine, to which I responded that I had no idea but that our Rotary had donated the first $250.00 to get us started. Without batting an eye, Dr. Phil offered to match what the Rotary was donating, and before we knew it, as much new underwear as $500 could ship was headed overseas. The rest stayed behind and was distributed locally to homeless shelters. Sometimes, all you need to do is ask.

Supplies for Our Soldiers (SOS): Every year for the past twelve years, we have remembered our soldiers on active duty with thank-you cards and letters. For the past five years, we've also included care packages. The soldiers get not only some basic-need items but also some pamper-yourself things so that they know we're thinking of them and thankful for them. And every year, we're shocked at the generosity of our school family and greater community. Our first year, we arrived at the post office with 129 boxes to ship. We knew what each box would cost and that each box needed a customs form. What we didn't know was that each box also needed the soldier's address written on the box along with our return address. As the USPS worker prepared and posted each box, a volunteer and I were frantically matching up information on customs forms with what we needed to write on boxes. Before we knew it, there were people lining up...to help us! Three of them even gave us monetary donations to help defray the cost of postage. One handed us a $100 bill and thanked us for remembering our servicemen and women. We were blown away by his generosity! Every year this project gets better and better. In November 2013, we sent forty-five boxes full of homemade goodness in the form of cookies and cookie bars. At ten dozen per box, we calculated that we'd baked approximately 5,400 tasty treats that were shipped out for our troops just in time for Thanksgiving. For our reflection piece, we invited the soldiers to visit us via Skype from their quarters or in person once they return.

SOUPer Bowl of Caring: Over the years, we've called our canned food drives by different names, like Wee Can or Feeding Our Friends. No matter what you call it, there's no project more important than tackling hunger by supporting your local pantries and helping put food on their shelves. This project can so easily transform from service (bring a can of corn) to service-learning (integrate the donation into curricular areas). Can students weigh the items? Sort them by size, shape, color? Compare and contrast nutritional values? Estimate costs? Do some research on the project? Match the items to the food pyramid? Create an advertising campaign for the goods? Share family favorite recipes? You CAN see that the extension possibilities seem endless...and the value added to the learning through this project, priceless.

Our Pet Project: Students love animals, which makes them the perfect medium by which to empower children to make a difference. And animals depend on us for survival, so this project enriches students' study of living organisms, as well as integrates information to help students become responsible pet owners, understand animal needs, and assist the animal population in our area. Invite local animal groups to partner with you to make this project come alive. We hosted representatives from Houston Collie Rescue and a wildlife expert who rehabs injured birds. (Note: The teacher will need to check on pet allergies prior to these visits.) Ask volunteers to bring an animal and discuss the needs of the pet, responsible pet ownership, safety around animals, and ways that students can help. Our partners left a poster with a picture of the "class pets" as a visual reminder of the animals in the community that need our help.

Not only do animals rely on us, but we also rely on them. There are many ways in which an animal can serve, hence the dog's nickname "man's best friend." Sadie, a trained reading dog, often helps with our small group counseling classes. Our Friendswood Police has a K-9 unit. People who have sight impairments use seeing-eye dogs. Horses are being used as therapy animals. Brainstorm with your class ways in which animals work for and with us. This piece can serve as a nice parallel between our value of responsibility and these animals. What is their responsibility toward us? What is ours toward them? A packet of additional activities can be downloaded from the American Kennel Club in the Responsible Dog Owner section at http://classic.akc.org/kids_juniors under the Dog Owners tab.

Throughout the unit of study, students can bring donations to support these groups in their efforts to help the animals. At the end, students can journal or videotape their reflections and write thank-you notes to the guests for their visit and/or to other organizations that care for animals.

A special thanks goes to master teachers Carolyn Lowe and Michelle Maruca for sharing their expertise on these extension ideas. Students can:

★ Collect data and chart their findings on the different breeds of dogs or other animals they know or would like to know more about, perhaps even their "class pet." Students could also conduct an independent research project on the domesticated animal of their choice.

★ Find or illustrate different pictures of dogs and cats. Students can then identify the different needs of the animals. For example, larger dogs need room to run, require more food, etc. This can be a class activity as well. All students who have pets can bring a picture and, as a class, compare and contrast needs through a Venn diagram, an H map, or a double-bubble graphic organizer.

★ Create an animal care diary for their "class pet." They can include a picture of the animal, the animal's breed or name, what the animal likes to eat, games it likes to play, when and where the animal needs to be fed, and what other special needs the breed might have. This is also the place where students could do research about what to do when animals need health care.

★ Use food brochures to find the cost of pet food. Students can discuss how much an animal needs to eat in a year and multiply to see how much food they will need to buy and then calculate the cost to feed an animal for a year.

★ Draw a *Wanted Poster* with animal needs around the picture (idea web). Students can use their idea web to write sentences to their parents and the community that teach them about their "class pet."

★ Write a persuasive letter to the community to convince someone to adopt their pet. The persuasive letter could also be addressed to an animal trainer asking him or her to donate some time to train stray animals. Well-behaved pets are easier to adopt!

★ Find a good book on animals, including storybooks about owning a dog (or cat), books about dogs that help people, and/ or reference books. Check out *Crash!* by Mayra Calvani, *Loving Marley* by Donald and Sara Hassler, and *Good News Nelson* by Jodi Moore. Or visit the library for other reading materials that you could use. Watch a film clip about responsible pet ownership during lunch or library time. Discuss the pros and cons of owning a pet.

★ Take a field trip to a local animal shelter so that students can visit with the animals. Find out if they have volunteer opportunities, like walking or brushing the animals.

Reaching Out Is "Sew" Much Fun: What do students in Friendswood, Texas, have in common with a women's shelter in Oklahoma? Fabric, accessories, measurements, and an awesome second grade teacher. When Laura Hunter pitched a win-win way to help stock the shelves of a store in Oklahoma, it hit a home run with our students. During guidance class, after students watched a video clip about a group of women who learn to sew and then sell their goods to make ends meet, they decided collectively that they would love to bring fabric, buttons, thread, needles, scissors, and other supplies to help these women out. Families donated a yard each of fun fabric prints and coordinating thread and notions so that these seamstresses could sew to support their families. This project joined us together knowing something seemingly so small would make such a big difference in the world of some women and their children whom we would likely never meet. Yep, superheroes know that serving others can be "sew" rewarding! We received not only letters of thanks from the women we helped but also a copy of the article about our partnership from the Bartlesville paper that we could read aloud to the students during our community gathering. Best of all, the women sent us a few hand-sewn aprons, which our cafeteria volunteers wear during lunch duty to this day. Service-learning opportunities greatly enhance our superheroes.

Chapter 2

U IS FOR UNCONDITIONAL LOVE

Superheroes must have an amazing capacity for love. Just think about it: they rush in to help, regardless of who needs them. They don't put any conditions on who, when, where, or how they help. They instinctively think with their hearts and not just feel love, either, but act on it. Superheroes are all about action.

I'll never forget Hailey. She was in third grade, but she'd decided she didn't want to knit. In fact, she came by my office to donate her needles and yarn to someone who did. She told me, in no uncertain terms, that she wasn't interested and lovingly added that she wanted someone else to have her stuff. As third grade went on and she saw her classmates making baby hats, Hailey stopped by to ask if I thought I could teach her to knit. She'd gotten some money for the holidays and thought she'd like to buy more needles and give it a shot. It was rough going at first, but Hailey eventually finished a beautiful little blue hat. When she was interviewed for our *Knit One, Save One* documentary, Hailey said, in her caring voice and with warmth in her eyes, "I knit this hat for a baby, and I knit this hat with love." No parameters, no conditions. Just love. She knit that hat with love. For a baby whom she'll never meet. She added that since she survived when she was a baby, those little babies should have the same chance.

On the home front, my son's sixth grade teacher, Autumn Bockart, puts love in motion like none other. You might know the feeling. You're in a meeting when the phone buzzes in your pocket or purse. You can't get outside quick enough and you miss a call from your child's school. You frantically try to call back, but you're not even sure who was calling in the first place. The counselor? The nurse? His teacher? The principal? Oh, please, not the principal! There's a beep while you're on the other line, trying to figure it out, that indicates whoever just called has left you a message.

It was Mrs. Bockart, and her message made me cry. Inside and out. A bit from relief, but mostly from the feeling of joy that washed over me. I seriously started sobbing because I could hear my son Joshua in the background. And I could feel his excitement and pride as she said, "I'm calling because today is 'I Love Joshua Day' in my classroom, and I just want to tell you what a fantastic kid he is and how much I enjoy having him in my class. He always smiles and always has a positive attitude and he always gives 110% and I couldn't ask for anything more." She went on to say that they were sorry that they'd missed me and that they hoped I enjoyed their message.

Joshua's teacher had made a thirty-second call that totally made my day. And talk about a win-win for my boy! His role model bragged to his mom and dad about him, explaining what makes him special and why she loves him. I didn't have to see his face to know that he was beaming from ear to ear. That night, Joshua said a prayer of thanks for Mrs. Bockart "'cause she finds the good in everyone." Then he added slyly, "Even if they're bad." No wonder she loves that kid!

This thoughtful, compassionate teacher weaves this amazing climate of caring into her classroom with planned acts of kindness, like taking the time to share that message with Joshua's number one fan, me. She teaches her students by example and helps them to be better every day, not only at reading and language arts but at smiling and staying positive, at trusting and loving, at being in the moment and being a good friend. Her small act went a very long way and rippled out in so many directions for me that afternoon. We carried "I Love Joshua Day" on into the night, of course, and have been looking for ways to pay it forward ever since.

Superheroes look for ways to pay it forward. To do one good thing. Do you know about the Power of One? Well, kindness begets kindness, and, just like the old Fabergé Organics Shampoo commercial that suggests you tell a friend and she'll tell a friend and so on and so on, if you do a kind thing every day and the recipient of that kindness does the same, do you know how many kind acts you'd have at the end of a short month, like February? 268,435,456. Even more for a month with 30 and 31 days! Katie Couric reminds us that, "We can't assume that kindness is an inherited trait; it is a learned behavior."[7] Unconditional love and kindness go hand in hand. Acts of kindness, random or planned, have a boomerang effect.

Perhaps you've seen blog posts about people who do Random Acts of Kindness (RAKs) in honor of their birthday. My friend Deanna decided to celebrate "sixty by sixty," completing sixty RAKs during her sixtieth birthday year. Here's what she told readers at my blog, The Corner on Character:

> *"I learned that it is not always easy being kind. I made some sacrifices to complete some of them, but from those sacrifices came wonderful blessings. I learned that it is in giving that we receive, and, more times than not, I was the one blessed...the most important thing I have taken away from this experience is that there are opportunities to be kind all around us, every day. It can be as simple as a smile or a kind word. We just have to take our eyes off of ourselves and put them on those around us."*

Use books like *One Smile* by Cindy McKinley, *Because Amelia Smiled* by David Ezra Stein, *Max's Magic Seeds* by Geraldine Elschner, *The Invisible Boy* by Trudy Ludwig, or *Each Kindness* by Jacqueline Woodson to talk about the domino effect of showing love by being kind. Then, using these lyrics, dance the Bunny Hop.

Here's how: Take two steps out to the side on the right, then two steps out to the side on the left, then jump forward one hop, jump backward one hop, and hop forward three times, like a bunny.

♪ *Do a kind act; it'll boomerang back.*
Give kind, get kind; just like that!

Here are some random, low-cost loving acts to consider:

★ Adopt a class in another state and make friendship bracelets for them.

★ Place phone calls or computer chats to wish grandparents of your students a "Happy Birthday" with a singing telegram.

★ Write blind affirmations and tape them around the school.

★ Host a "Yappy Hour" and let pet owners bring their pets for students to play with, groom, and walk.

★ Put a nice note inside of a popular library book for the next person who checks it out.

★ Encourage students to find a new friend to sit with at lunch.

★ Help your students write a thank-you note to a former teacher.

★ Decorate placemats with a character message to distribute at local restaurants.

★ Let students write positive, uplifting messages for the school marquee.

★ Write thank-you notes to your parents and put them in the mail.

The Most Valuable A's Students Can Earn

Over the years, children have attended school to learn the three all-important R's—Reading, wRiting, and aRithmetic. I propose that students learn three equally valuable A's—Affirmation, Appreciation, and Apology. These values are as effectively "caught as taught," so first and foremost, we must lead by example. For the first A, affirmation, here are some questions for you to consider:

★ Whom have you affirmed lately?

★ How do you encourage affirmations in your classroom?

★ Are you practicing how to sincerely compliment one another with your students?

★ Do you provide opportunities for students to dig beneath the surface and truly notice each other's superpowers?

★ How about using drops in a bucket, a compliment notebook, or an affirmation take-home journal?

The second coveted A is appreciation. Start by finding ways to thank your students and their parents. When you show appreciation, guess what happens? Students want to show appreciation, too. You just have to teach them how. Show them how to write a thank-you note and give them time to write them to parents, grandparents, a counselor, or a former teacher. Turn this into a writing center activity and have blank thank-you notes available. Students can create them every day for everyday people with community service jobs that sometimes go unappreciated such as the mail carrier, a police officer, a firefighter, a garbage collector, or a grocery store cashier. Then sit back and enjoy the radiance of the sunshine they'll be spreading.

The third A is apology. Superheroes show love by apologizing. Teach your students to take responsibility for their actions by saying, "I did it. I'm sorry. Please forgive me." Then have them fix it and move on. Students also have to learn to accept an apology. Let them know that rather than saying, "It's okay," they should consider saying, "I forgive you." We role-play this a lot in my office because a genuine apology is critical to emotional health and well-being. Maybe you've heard about or participated in the activity where you carry around a small sack of potatoes for a week to represent something you need to apologize for or forgive. You're charged with taking the sack with you everywhere you go, never putting it down. This serves as a nice metaphor about how cumbersome and eventually rotten grudges and guilt can become. Instead, the next time you mess up, give yourself an A and apologize. Then practice it over and over again with your students.

In my thirty years of education, one of the most loving, kind, and generous people I've met is Mary, a registrar from my days at Friendswood High School. She moved out into the country a few years back, but she's still near and dear to my heart. Every time I visit, she's feeding some new critters. Birds. Raccoons. Honeybees. I love visiting her because it's like being home. My friends Mary and Wendy took me in for six months since I didn't have a place to stay between engagement and marriage. Mary naturally said I could stay with them, to help me out and because love is her superpower. I got to sleep in their beautifully dressed antique guest bedroom, on her granny's bed, while I planned the wedding and did some substitute teaching to make ends meet. I loved being adopted by Mary; it was a glorious time.

When our children were born, there wasn't any family close by, and Mary was one of the only people I'd leave them with, so we adopted her. She's been Aunt Mary to us ever since. And, as you might imagine, she was our best babysitter ever. And she did it all at no charge. All of it.

The Beatles were on to something when they sang their ballad that claimed, "All you need is love." Love for humankind. Without conditions. Just because we care and we can. I fondly remember this interaction with Michael, a pint-sized first grader with the biggest heart under his character cape.

This particular wave of love started with a little ripple when this wide-eyed boy stopped by my office, like he often does, for a quick hello. The raspy quality of his voice still echoes in my mind as I replay the urgency of his earnest request.

"Mrs. Gruener, you know those poor people who were hurt by that killer wave?"

Picturing the devastation I'd seen on the news following that horrific tsunami, I knowingly nodded, never expecting what came next.

"We're going to help them, aren't we?" he confidently added.

Many thoughts started swimming through my head as I struggled to find the words to gently tell Michael that no, since we just sent School Supply Kits to Iraqi children and since we were about to launch our quarters collection for the fully integrated playground project, and since lots of people worldwide were already helping the tsunami victims, we probably would not be taking on another service project right now. But instead of any of that, I felt myself smile and heard myself tell Michael, "That's a great idea! What did you have in mind?"

We began our first student-initiated collection. We would ask our students to find a way to earn a dollar this week. Maybe there's a chore that they could do for their parents or family friends, or maybe there's a need that they could fill to earn that cash. They would bring their dollar on Friday, for the one-day collection we'd call **100 Cents for Tsunami Survivors**. As a visible reminder of this precious opportunity to create a wave of love in this way, an empty five-gallon water jug would hold their donations. If everyone participated, our $800 donation would surely make a difference to the UNICEF relief efforts.

From a ripple came the wave of heartwarming tales. Students lined up with coin purses, wallets, and piggy banks filled with pennies, quarters, and dollar bills, ready to show their support by filling the jug. There was a third grade boy who gave most of the allowance money in his wallet. There was a first grade girl who donated all of the money she'd earned for her report card. There was a second grade boy who emptied his piggy bank to donate his entire savings. A kindergarten boy and his third grade sister baked cookies with their mom and sold them to bring in a sizable donation. Another second grade boy helped his friends raise money by selling lemonade on the corner. And a first grade boy wrote a poem about how we're ready to help the tsunami children, ending it with "ready or not, here I come!" Such generosity almost doubled our initial goal, and our school family sent just over $1,500 to UNICEF. I'm amazed at the natural power generated by kids helping kids, and I will always hold heartfelt gratitude to Michael for stopping by my office that day and causing the ripple effect that created this incredible wave of love.

From that interaction, I wrote these lyrics that we sing to the tune of Nick Lowe's song "Cruel to Be Kind":

It's so cool to be kind, it starts right here with me.
Just cool to be kind; sprinkle kindness and see.
Way cool to be kind, and peacemakers are we.
Hey friends, it really is cool to be kind!

We are richly blessed to be in a position to dynamically shape the hearts of our superheroes and teach them to love and be loved so that they can continue to use their superpowers for good.

Chapter 3

P IS FOR PERSEVERANCE

While I like the word "perseverance" and everything that it's associated with, I much prefer a word that my great aunt Norma coined for me at a very young age: stick-to-it-tiveness. She told my dad that I had the most stick-to-it-tiveness that she'd ever seen. Later, my aunt Eileen said that she'd said that about her, too. In any event, I liked that word a lot and was very proud to be good at something called stick-to-it-tiveness. The evidence that Aunt Norma had was this: on the weekends when I went to her house after school on a Friday, we'd play piano duets until we could barely get ourselves up the steps to bed. Then, the minute I'd smell the coffee brewing, I'd come back downstairs and tickle the ivories until it was time for her to walk me home. It was heaven on earth, to spend that time with Aunt Norma. Not only was she my great aunt, she was also my first and second grade teacher. In fact, she taught for fifty years before retiring. She modeled the superpower of perseverance by spending more than half of her life in a classroom, nurturing hearts and minds for the future as well as all of those hours with me so I could learn how to make music at the piano and the organ. From it, I learned to not give up on something just because it was difficult at first, or stretched and/or challenged me. Turns out that I handed down that trait to my daughter, Kaitlyn. She actually won a national essay contest for her thoughts about her attitude and stick-to-it-tiveness, as well as five thousand dollars and a lawnmower for her school.

Here now, the Foundations for Life essay from which she adapted her entry:

It's All about Attitude by Kaitlyn Gruener (8th grade)
Foundations for Life Essay Contest Maxim: "Whether you think you can or not, you are right."—Henry Ford[8]

During seventh grade, in my construction careers class, we watched a documentary of the life of the great Henry Ford, founder of the Ford Motor Company. During the film, this quote jumped out at me. Even though it was an incidental part of the movie, it grabbed my attention because I realized how true this was. Upon receiving the quote list for this year, I spotted this quote. It reminded me of the video last year, and I knew that I needed to choose this particular maxim for this reflective essay.

This quote relates to my life in so many ways. I am the pitcher on my 14U A-ball fast-pitch softball team. My pitching coach gives me weekly tests to see how I am improving. If I don't pass the task, I must retake it the next week until I have mastery over that aspect. One test, nicknamed the distractions test, was designed to see how well I could block out annoying and distracting noises while on the pitching mound. My coach would talk to me, sneeze, cough, jump up and down, and do other things to distract me from throwing strikes. It took me 52 weeks, a whole year, to pass this task, longer than it had taken anyone else. I would repeatedly fail the distractions test week after week, until I finally realized something. I was always going into the lessons saying, "There's no way I'm going to pass this test." My attitude toward the test was negative and pessimistic, and I believed I couldn't pass it. I never even once said, "I can do this," or "I will pass this test." I had been limiting myself to failure. After my enlightenment, I approached the test with a positive attitude and the belief that I could achieve this goal, and I finally passed the lesson. I know it sounds unbelievable, but I passed.

Because of telling myself, "I can do it," instead of, "I can't," I was able to overcome an obstacle that troubled me for a long time.

Another example of this quote's relevance to my life is in academics. Being in Geometry, math at a level two years advanced for my age, is very difficult. It requires a lot of effort and a positive mentality. Taking tests on this material is stressful for me, and sometimes my stress turns into negative comments, such as, "I can't do this," and "It's way too hard for me." Even after studying hard for a test, if my attitude is pessimistic, it will cause me to be so nervous that I'll forget all the things I studied. On a test not too long ago, I was worrying so badly and putting myself down with comments like, "I'm going to fail." Although my friends said that I would do fine, they were wrong. As soon as I set my mind to thinking that I was going to fail, I had doomed myself to do badly. I got an 83 on that test, and because of my high expectations, it was an unacceptable grade. I had set myself up to be knocked down. Even with the proper studying, my bad attitude had caused me to get a bad grade on a test that would count for a lot. On the next test, my attitude was great, and I believed in myself, that I had the ability to make a good grade. I had also studied again, but no more than on the test before. Sure enough, I got a 100. My teacher stopped me in the hall that morning before my class to tell me she was proud of me. I was proud of myself, too. It just goes to show that your attitude really does matter.

My attitude also plays an important part in my music. I play the clarinet, and last year at Region Band tryouts, I did not even place in the District Band, the lowest, non-performing band. Going to Region tryouts this year, my mom told me to do my best, to which I replied, "What if my best isn't good enough?" I doubted myself, thinking that I wouldn't make it, even if I tried my best. It was the same self-doubt I had encountered during the distractions and math tests. I knew I needed to overcome it, and I wasn't about to let it get the best of me again. With positive thoughts, my confidence grew as I patiently waited for my turn. At the end of the day, when they were announcing results, I saw that I had placed 6th out of 115 clarinet players. I had made Symphonic Region Band, the best band I could achieve. Only the top players get to go to

Region Orchestra, the highest honor for a junior high band student, and when I was chosen as an alternate, I knew I had made a breakthrough in overcoming my attitude and self-doubt issues.

An attitude does not just influence how you do on tests. It helps you make decisions in everyday life. One of my favorite books when I was little was **The Little Engine That Could** by Watty Piper. In that story, the little engine is trying to climb up a hill. She tries and tries and tries, but since she doesn't believe she'll make it, she struggles. However, once she starts saying, "I think I can, I think I can" she makes it up and over the hill to deliver her goods. Because of her positive attitude toward her abilities and what she can do, she can suddenly do more things than ever!

Henry Ford's quote has inspired me to keep a positive attitude toward life. This concept has made a difference in my life. "Whether you think you can or not, you are right," seems too simple, but in reality it's not. If you set your sights high, whatever you believe, you can achieve. It's all about attitude.

In each of Kaitlyn's examples, changing her mindset helped her persevere. How many teens do you know that'll stick with something, actually be stuck on it, for fifty-two weeks, a full year, without giving up? That's what superheroes with perseverance do. They must internally do a cost-benefit analysis. Learning new skills is hard. Becoming a leader is hard. Life is hard. And sometimes it costs more than someone is willing to pay. But when you stick with something, there's typically a benefit, the light at the end of that tunnel that'll shine within to say "job well done!"

How could you use this story and/or a lesson like this to encourage your students to share who they are and what they value? Write a weekly quote on the whiteboard and see who notices. Or have them mull it over during your morning meeting or sensitivity circle. Host an essay contest like the one Kaitlyn entered. Or use maxims as writing prompts to help students sharpen their critical thinking skills. Hang popular posters that say things like "Winners never quit and quitters never win." See what your students have to say about them. Do they believe that to be true? If not, what might be a better way to encourage perseverance? Send them on an assignment to bring in quotes that speak to them and would likely spark a discussion with their peers. Discuss them in class meetings.

Most of you are probably familiar with Aesop's fable *The Tortoise and the Hare.* This is the story about the quickness of a rabbit versus the slow-and-steady, methodical ways of the turtle. While there are different versions of this tale, the tortoise's perseverance on the path trumps the rabbit's sprint with distractions to the finish line. Journeying down the character road is more of a marathon than a sprint. We are in training every day to be in the right place at the right time, doing the right thing, just like the tortoise. Steven Covey advised, "Begin with the end in mind,"[9] which the hare started out doing, but he lost sight of the end because of his lack of focus and stick-to-it-tiveness.

So, how do we get our superheroes to stay the course? They have to have permission to fail. They need to know that not only is failure okay but that, according to author Paul Tough, it might be the key to success. In his research, Tough found that grit, resilience, and perseverance were key ingredients in the success stories of their test subjects.[10] Kids who don't give up when they encounter obstacles in their way, who don't quit when they hit a pothole in the road, and who don't abandon ship when the winds shift and steering their vessel seems all but impossible are the kids who find the greatest success through their school years and beyond. As we coach these learners, we must encourage them to take risks and to be okay with messing up. They need to know that mistakes are opportunities for reflection, improvement, and growth. We must help them strive to do THEIR best, not be THE best. We have to change the mindset that the silver medal is somehow losing. Silver isn't losing. It's coming in second. That's all. When did silver get so tarnished? Is it possible that we're raising kids to quit when they think they can't attain the coveted gold at the end of the rainbow? When my daughter started in the marching band, she had high hopes for them at the State Marching Contest. They were marching a clean and elegant show with strong music, and they ended up fourth in the State of Texas out of 250 bands their size. Two years and lots of growth and improvement later, their band came out of the preliminary competition number one. But there were still finals with new judges and a clean slate. The students marched their hearts out, and they came in second. They were devastated. Crushed to have gotten so close to gold and yet so far. Second place out of so many bands is good, no doubt, but they set their standards high. They worked hard, and there was a lot of disappointment.

But here's what superheroes know: winning is a state of mind. There were thousands of students who didn't even get a trip to the state competition because they didn't advance out of their district or their area, so just getting to state made them winners. The way that the 271 members, musicians and guard members, together created magic with their music made them winners. Leaving it all on the field, heart and soul, made them winners. It shouldn't matter, if they worked hard, persevered, and gave it their best, and earned second or fifth or tenth.

There are exemplary examples of perseverance in history, too. Commander-in-Chief George Washington persevered with his ragtag army of militiamen in his fight against the British for American Independence for six years.[11] President Abraham Lincoln persevered to preserve the union and free the slaves.[12] Senator John McCain spent over five years as a prisoner of war in Vietnam.[13] He persevered through horrible conditions and survived to tell about it. Helen Keller persevered through a childhood illness that left her deaf and blind.[14] Astronaut Sally Ride persevered through a male-dominated field to become the first American woman astronaut to travel into outer space.[15] Figure skater Nancy Kerrigan, though badly injured, worked hard to regain her strength and persevered through the pain to earn the silver medal.[16] And the list goes on and on. There is rich value when students study heroes in history, not only for solid examples of perseverance but for other admirable character virtues and traits.

As a young girl, I often heard my father recite this poem:

> *When a job has once begun, never leave it 'til it's done.*
> *Be it big or be it small; do it right or not at all.*[17]

I didn't understand its importance and significance as a child, necessarily, but it certainly rings true over and over again. Teach it in your poetry unit.

You'll also find examples of perseverance in picture books like *Leo the Lightning Bug* by Eric Drachman, *Leo the Late Bloomer* by Robert Kraus, *The Little Firefly* by Sheri Fink, or *Dream Big, Little Pig* by Kristi Yamaguchi. Talk with your students about enduring through obstacles and moving steadfastly forward despite difficulties. Ask students to talk, write, or draw about a time that something got too hard and they thought about just giving up. What happened? What was that experience like? What made them decide to stick it out? How did it feel when it was all over? Ask them to compare that time to one of these stories or another one that they've read that deals with perseverance. Have them write a "Dear Abby" response letter giving their advice to the main character.

Finally, ask your students if there's ever a time when quitting would be okay, maybe even the best thing to do. How do they know when that is? Who are the people who can help them with those difficult decisions?

Then, stick to it. Keep on keeping on. As Newt Gringrich said, "Perseverance is the hard work you do after you get tired of doing the hard work you already did."[18]

Chapter 4

E IS FOR EMPATHY

Ah, the glorious virtue of empathy. The ability to switch places with someone, to put yourself in their shoes. To understand what they're experiencing and feel what they're feeling. This abstract concept can be difficult for our younger superheroes to wrap their minds around, so laying the groundwork in the cognitive domain is important. Make "empathy" a verb and flood their world with it. I weave it into every single lesson that I do in peace class (formerly known as guidance class). We even have a silent symbol for that big important word. Try it; it's easy. Making fists out of your hands, put your thumb up on the left hand and pinky finger up on the right hand. Now, switch places. On the left, pull the thumb in and put the pinky up at the same time that you put the thumb up and pull the pinky in on the right. Then switch again. Simultaneously. As they master the switch, have them recite this little poem I wrote:

It's empathy. It's empathy.
When you put yourself
in place of me,
it's empathy.

When students encounter an experience that elevates their empathy, they'll give me the silent-symbol switch. There isn't a book on my shelf in which you can't switch places with a character and feel what they're feeling. That's why it comes up every time we get together. Children who read fiction have higher levels of empathy; the more students read, the more opportunities they have to learn about, experience, and embrace empathy. And guess what? Students whose empathy has been nurtured and stretched are less likely to exhibit bullying behaviors and more likely to stand up and step in when bullying behaviors surface.

Let's look at one of my favorite lessons, adapted from an idea shared by Tanya Kirschman, a counseling colleague in Montana. All it takes is a few pairs of shoes and some stories. Write your own or use the ones I wrote. I used a pair of toddler high tops, a pair of boy's slippers, and some women's sneakers. Put the shoes in a shoebox and paste these scenarios onto the box top. Let students pick the box they want and hold the shoes or put them on. Encourage them to experience how it feels to wear someone else's shoes while you read that person's story aloud.

I am a nine-month-old baby and something's wrong so I'm going to the doctor. I haven't been sleeping well, so I've been kind of fussy lately. It could be that I'm cutting some teeth, but Mom's not sure. I want to stop crying, but it's really hard. I'm too young to explain how I'm feeling because I don't talk yet. What do you think I need? What do you think my mom needs? How are we feeling? How could you use your superpower to help us?

———— ★ ————

I am staying home today because I have a tummy ache. Actually, I just moved this summer because Mom and Dad broke up, and I don't like my new school because I don't feel safe there yet. I really wish I could go back to my other school! This is my third day to miss school so far and my mom says she'll get fired if she has to keep taking off of work to stay home with me. Put yourself in my shoes. What do you think is going on with me? How can I fit in better at my new school so these butterflies in my tummy go away? What do I need? What does my mom need? What superpower would you need to help me?

———— ★ ————

I am the mom of one little girl and we're homeless right now. It's not like we're living on the streets, though. We're in this nice program where we get to live at a church for two weeks before we have to go to another church. The people feed us and we have a place to sleep and shower. I used to be a librarian but I don't have a job now, so I'm looking for work so that I can find somewhere for us to live and be able to pay the bills. Put yourself in place of me. How do I feel? What do I need? What does my daughter need? How could you help us with your superpower?

The discussion that follows will amaze you, but expect things like the baby needs a rattle, the boy needs some medicine, the daughter needs a dog. No answer is incorrect here, and these developmentally appropriate, concrete responses are a great starting point. You'll need to encourage students to keep thinking, to go deeper with questions such as the following:

★ What else might these people need?

★ Why might they need more than just the surface, tangible things?

★ Why might the dog be a good idea?

★ Is there something about the responsibilities of a pet that makes it a bad idea for the girl and her mom right now?

★ Might there be a better time for them to adopt a dog?

Then have the students write their own scenarios, either from real-life experiences or imagined, and see what happens. A blog reader suggested maybe even leaving one box empty with a scenario in which the person doesn't even have any shoes. I predict you'll find this exercise a good fit in your quest to elevate empathy.

After this lesson, a kindergarten boy with special needs went back to class and got frustrated about something. Unable to clearly verbalize what he wanted, he shouted at his teacher and, as a consequence, had to change his behavior chart color. After he calmed down and was processing what had happened, he demanded from his teacher, "Why can't you practice empathy on me?" At five years old, he was working to understand and learn that vocabulary and subsequently used it in the right context.

A book that we use to move from cognitive to the affective domain is *Those Shoes* by Maribeth Boelts. This book speaks to us because there's a well-intentioned counselor in the story who gives Jeremy, a little boy in need, some shoes. But, unlike the ones he's got his eye on, they're actually pretty dorky, with a Bob-the-Builder type character on them. In a stroke-of-luck moment, however, Jeremy does find the shoes he wants at a resale shop, but they aren't quite his size. What he does with them after he realizes that they aren't ever going to fit is what endears this tale to me. After reading this story aloud and checking for comprehension, ask your students:

★ When was the last time you put yourself in someone else's shoes?

★ What happened?

★ What was that experience like?

★ What was easy about it?

★ What was burdensome?

★ How did it feel?

After the reading and discussion, take a brain break by singing the following poem and dancing it to the tune and moves of the Bunny Hop:

🎼 E–M–P–A–T–H–Y,
put yourself in my place,
c'mon, give it a try.
E–M–P–A–T–H–Y,
'cause if you feel what I feel
you might understand why.

Use technology to talk more about empathy by searching for the adorable Mark Ruffalo and Murray Sesame Street video online.

So, you get your students to embrace empathy; then what? They need to see you showing empathy and be encouraged to look for examples of it in real life. Process movies or television shows with them when they're over. How would you like to trade places with that main character? What would it be like? What would you want to stay the same? What would you want to change?

Once they've embraced it, it's time to bring this virtue to life, to give students an opportunity to practice it, like my brother Mark does. Mark puts empathy into action every time a heavy snow hits Milwaukee. I'm not sure how he happened into that job and I don't think he's always had it, but he's become the resident snow blower on his street. I vaguely remember a time, actually, when he used a good old-fashioned shovel and it was all he could do to clear his own drive. Maybe it was when he got the monster machine that allows him to throw snow like it's sand. Or quite possibly it's because he himself cannot stand the thought of being snow-bound, so he wants to help keep his neighbors from being snowed in as well. Regardless of his motivation, like a good neighbor, my brother's there. One year, they got twenty inches of the powdery white stuff and he spent five hours behind his blower. One hour on his drive, four hours on the neighboring sidewalks and driveways. I'm guessing it's kind of fun, in a weird sort of way, or he wouldn't have braved the frozen tundra temps to give such a gift. He puts himself in their "boots" and layers on his orange reflective hunting clothes. He fires up his 30" Craftsman and blazes the trail to move the frozen flakes out of the way so that life can go on for his neighbors and friends.

And in the end, Mark seems to benefit as much from providing this severe-weather service as the recipients of his kindness do. It's not likely that we'll ever get that kind of snow in Texas, but if we do, I'd happily welcome a neighbor with empathy and a snow blower.

Now it's our students' turn:

★ What can they do to move empathy to the behavioral domain like Mark does?

Challenge them to seize opportunities for moral growth:

★ Who might appreciate their leaves being raked?

★ Or their car being washed?

★ Who might benefit from their dog being taken for a walk?

★ Or from having a freshly baked treat delivered?

There are so many things that students can do. Depending on age, all they need is a ride and/or some supervision. Using their empathy switch and trading places with the custodians, would the school bathrooms be cleaner? Thinking about the environment, what could they do during recess that'd make a difference? What might their mom or dad want or need? How about a sibling or the new kid in class? Their teacher? How about a friend?

Empathy can serve as a powerful antidote to conflicts; who is someone they might be at odds with that might benefit from the gift of empathy? For our upper elementary-aged learners, share *The Sandal Artist* by Kathleen Pelley. The people in the town ask Roberto, a budding artist, to paint pictures of them, but Roberto tells them that he needs to paint extraordinary things, not ordinary things. In search of those beautiful things to paint, Roberto overlooks the beauty in everyday things around him. When he earns enough money and is able to get his own shoes resoled, Roberto experiences walking in another man's shoes and sees the same everyday things through someone else's lens with a very different end result.

Four other titles that should grace your shelves with a strong empathy theme include: *Four Feet, Two Sandals* by Karen Lynn Williams, *One Thousand Tracings: Healing the Wounds of World War II* by Lita Judge, *Stand in My Shoes: Kids Learning About Empathy* by Bob Sornson, PhD, and *The Orange Shoes* by Trinka Hakes Nobel.

After sharing these titles, take your empathy experts into the library and encourage them to select a story that has a strong example of understanding one another's situations and feeling what they're feeling by walking in their shoes. Stretch and nurture this important virtue and your superheroes will better understand one another and, in return, themselves.

Chapter 5

R IS FOR RESPECT

It's golden; treat others the way you want to be treated, the essence of the value of respect. You've got to give it to get it. It's circular that way; get it? At least twelve cultures ascribe to a variation of this mantra.

A few of them from the website www.teachingvalues.com[19] include:

Buddhism: Hurt not others in ways you yourself would find hurtful.

Christianity: In everything, do to others as you would have them do to you.

Confucianism: Do not unto others what you do not want them to do to you.

Hinduism: Do naught unto others which would cause you pain if done to you.

Islam: Not one of you is a believer until he loves for his brother what he loves for himself.

Judaism: What is hateful to you, do not do to your neighbor.

Taoism: Regard your neighbor's gain as your own gain and your neighbor's loss as your own loss.

Another version I've heard puts an interesting spin on it: May I be treated tomorrow how I treated people today.

What the rule doesn't do is work backward, in retribution: You treated me badly so I'm going to treat you badly now. We must teach our superheroes what respect looks like so they can imitate it.

And before our littlest learners understand respect, we must pair tangible behaviors with our abstract words. We need to show them how respect looks, sounds, and feels through modeling, seizing teachable moments, pointing out respect when we see it, and giving students many, many opportunities to practice their courtesy, manners, and kindness. Think about how we learned to say "please." When we're learning about the power of language and we have a request, adults in our lives will ask, "What's the magic word?" It's an if-then situation. If you say "please," then you typically get what you want. Over time, a pause replaces the question. And before long, no pause required. We move from knowing it to loving it to doing it.

When it moves from cognitive to affective and we feel it, then it starts to become real. But respect won't happen in isolation; it happens when we witness and experience it in action. When we weave it as a habit into our daily routines and are able to show it authentically in real-life situations, then it's a part of who we are and how we behave.

Try teaching the concept of respect using this ditty with the hand jive.

The hand-jive moves include two pats on your legs, two claps, slide hands right to left, then left to right, pound fists twice, then switch and pound fists two more times, then thumbs up right followed by thumbs up left, both over the shoulder.

🎼 R-E-S-P-E-C-T
We've got to give it, to get it;
yeah, that's the key.
We live by the golden rule, you see,
at (insert your school name here) Elementary.

Students love to chant, recite, and/or dance this. Start out slowly and let students speed it up as they're able.

I first found the picture book *Hey, Little Ant* by Phillip and Hannah Hoose back in the year 2000 when I moved from working with teens to working with middle school students. It has the power to single-handedly take its readers through all the domains of character, from cognitive to affective and ultimately to behavioral and back. Through a rhyming and respectful conversation between an ant and a child, this masterpiece tackles the question "to squish or not to squish" and ends in a classic question (cue the Golden Rule): "If you were me and I were you, what would you want me to do?"

Follow up and enrich this gem with the following ideas:

★ Are the child and the ant equal? Why or why not?

★ Would it be fair for the child to squish the ant?

★ If they were to trade places, would the ant squish the child? Why or why not?

★ Are there people in your life that might treat you like a little ant?

★ Can you share a time when that happened to you? What did you do?

★ What can you do when someone tries to make you feel smaller than they are?

★ What can you do to make sure that you do not treat others like little ants?

★ Do you think that the child should squish the ant?

★ What if the ant were a mosquito? Bumblebee? Snake? Other insect or animal?

★ Who are the ants in your life that might squish you with their behaviors or bite you with their words?

From Whose Point of View?

Everyone has an opinion that is his/her point of view. This book can serve as an excellent opportunity to teach children about their points of view and where opinions and points of view originate. It can also springboard a lesson to guide children to base their opinions, or points of view, on their superhero values.

Divide your students by viewpoint. One group will be for students who share the child's point of view and the other is for students who share the ant's point of view. Ask the following questions to facilitate a debate:

★ Why do you think the child should squish the ant?

★ Why do you think the child should not squish the ant?

★ If the child does squish the ant, what might happen next?

★ If the child lets the ant go, then what might happen?

★ Could the child and the ant actually be friends? How?

Using superpowers as a guide, help students share their points of view on other topics. Use recycling, for example, or volunteering. Give them a statement like "Everybody should recycle" and have them share their opinions. Prompt their responses by asking questions about respect, citizenship, and caring. To further illustrate point of view, have students draw something from different points of view. For example, how would a pencil look if you were an ant? What does your town look like to a bird? Have them draw three views of a common everyday object, like their toothbrush.

To Squish or Not to Squish?

Individually, or in small groups of three or four, have the children continue the dialogue between the child and the ant by writing the next two verses of the story. This will allow them to take a look at their sense of respect, justice, and fairness as they decide in which direction the ending should go.

Decisions, Decisions

Using the whiteboard or large flip-chart paper, make two columns for the groups. Write the word "squish" at the top left and "don't squish" at the top right. Using the book, review the arguments that the child and the ant each make. For example, the child is bigger and more powerful, so write "big and/or powerful" in the "squish" column. The ant contends that he is important to his community, so write "needed and/or important" in the "don't squish" column.

Continue until you have listed all of the points they make. Then have the children assign a smiley face to points that they see as important (pros) and a frowny face to points that they deem unimportant (cons). Encourage students to respectfully discuss and negotiate for each smile or frown. For example, some might think that being powerful is worth a smiley face, while others might not. Prompt them to think about their values as a guide: would it be fair to use your size to take advantage of someone who is smaller or weaker?

When the students list the "everybody's doing it," ask if superheroes allow their friends to pressure them into doing something or if it's better to stand up for what they believe in.

Does the kid show integrity if he allows peer pressure to help him make his decision? When they list the fact that the ant is needed to help feed nest mates, play devil's advocate and ask what the ant's argument says about its loyalty to family and its part as a citizen of the ant family. Try to get a consensus, or take a vote to show the students visually how to make solid decisions as a team.

At the end of the brainstorming session, look at the smiley faces for what seems important to the group. Notice if the column that has more happy faces is the better choice.

Explain that sometimes with dilemmas and decisions there isn't a simple answer or clear choice. This strategy can be a useful way to try to make decisions clearer and easier. To extend this lesson, have the students think of a time that they had a tough decision to make and have them sketch out on their papers what the two sides were and the pros and cons of each. Let them discuss this with a class partner, something we like to call buddy buzz.

Bully Busters

Respect is a great antidote for bullying. In the ant's world, the child's behaviors would be considered bullying behaviors because they're repeated, they're intentional, they're meant to threaten, and they create a huge power imbalance. Children with bullying behaviors tease and threaten others for a number of reasons, including but not limited to size, accent, skin color, nationality, religious beliefs, socioeconomic status, intelligence, or even their character and values that they hold dear. Superheroes stand up for who they are and what they believe in; they wear their character like a badge of honor with pride. Use the following inquiries as conversation starters or essay prompts.

★ Have you ever bullied anyone? Can you explain when and what happened?

★ Talk about a time you were bullied. Was the child who bullied bigger than you? Older? More courageous? Smarter? Stronger?

★ What are some of the differences that students who bully target?

★ What can you do if you are being bullied?

★ What is the difference between tattling and reporting?

★ What is it about our differences that can be so scary?

★ What can you do to make someone's differences less frightening?

Reinforce the Golden Rule and remind students how the ant used it to plead for its life. Encourage students to adopt this rule as their personal mantra. Show them that Martin Luther King, Jr.'s dream really is possible; that we should judge others by what's on the inside rather than what's on the outside and that we ought to value and honor all people from all walks of life.

Seal the deal by singing these lyrics while you dance the Chicken Dance:

𝄞 *(Beak) If a bully bothers you,*
(Wings) And you don't know what to do,
(Tail) Out at recess or in school,
Talk, Walk, then Tell (clap 4X).
I'll be a buddy, not a bully.
I'll be a friend and take a stand.
I'll jump in or go get a grownup,
so we can all lend a helping hand.

Other books that dovetail the value of respect beautifully include *Bird Child* by Nan Forler, *You're Mean, Lily Jean!* by Frieda Wishinsky, *The Band-Aid Chicken: A Program about Resisting Peer Pressure* by Becky Rangel Henton, *One* by Kathryn Otoshi, and *Spaghetti in a Hot Dog Bun: Having the Courage to Be Who You Are* by Maria Dismondy.

Children who show respect are peacemakers. Ask your students what they think makes someone a peacemaker. Let them make a list of peacemaking behaviors; they'll know what kinds of things they can do that will help keep the peace. Chart the behaviors and you'll have created a classroom constitution that will help you cultivate a culture of respect with your superheroes. Want to show it visually? Have a student lie down while you trace around him or her. On the inside of the tracing, ask them to draw and write what makes them feel respected and at peace. On the outside of the tracing, have them write or draw the things that keep them from feeling at peace, the stuff of the world that shows bad manners, rudeness, and disrespect. After a riveting discussion, ask them to cut it out. Literally cut around the edges and throw away the bad stuff, keeping the good stuff as a visual representation of how respect looks, sounds, and feels. Have students sign it with a thumbprint, their unique promise to uphold the contract.

The Golden Rule encapsulates the value of respect; keep it in the forefront by seizing teachable moments and giving students frequent opportunities to treat one another the way they want to be treated. Like kindness, respect has a boomerang effect. Give it away and watch how quickly it comes back.

Chapter 6

H IS FOR HONESTY

I was never as excited about my middle child's college choice as when we went on his summer orientation visit and they shared the Texas A & M Code of Honor with us: "An Aggie does not lie, cheat, steal, or tolerate those who do." Wow. Character values woven right into the fabric of who they are. Superheroes are honorable; they tell the truth.

Let's be honest—honesty is a must for any healthy friendship to stand a chance and survive. George Bernard Shaw once said, "The liar's punishment isn't in the least that he is not believed but that he cannot believe anybody else."[20] And it's true. Honest people can be trusted because they tell the truth. They keep their promises and we can count on them. Honest people don't do these things so that they won't get in trouble. They do these things because they're the right thing to do. Honest people live life with integrity.

The Empty Pot by Demi is a Chinese folktale that clearly illustrates the importance of telling the truth. In this book, the wise emperor is growing old and must choose a replacement for his crown. The flower-loving ruler announces that each child will be given a seed to see who can grow the most beautiful flower. His successor will be the most successful gardener in this challenge. Ping, a young villager known for his green thumb, is certain he can grow a great flower for the emperor. Despite his attentive care, Ping's seed will not grow. He problem-solves and tries a bigger pot and different soil but to no avail. When the day finally arrives and the emperor orders all of the children to bring their flowers to be inspected, Ping is ashamed to see so many children with their beautiful flowers. He has nothing to show the emperor but his empty pot. (One of my little listeners once asked me, "Why doesn't he just go to Walmart and buy some flowers?" Talk about foreshadowing!) His father assures him that he has tried his best, and his best is good enough.

The emperor looks with disappointment at the beautiful flowers before him. At last he approaches Ping and asks why his pot is empty. Ping explains that he did his best to grow the flower, but it just would not grow. Then the emperor smiles and exclaims that he has found his replacement. Who? And why?

This book is not one that you want to read straight through. Stop at different spots in the narrative to ask comprehension and cognition questions like:

★ What did Ping think about the contest at the beginning of the story?

★ Had Ping tried his best to get the seed to grow? How can you tell?

★ Does Ping ever give up and stop trying? How do you know?

★ Why doesn't Ping just go out and buy a fully grown bouquet of flowers?

★ Do you think Ping's father gave him good advice? Why or why not?

★ What's the difference between doing your best and being the best?

★ Why do you think the emperor seems unhappy with all the beautiful plants?

★ What had the emperor done? Why?

★ Do you think his "tricky" challenge seemed dishonest?

★ Who do you think is the best choice for emperor? Why?

★ What is integrity?

★ What do we mean when we say Ping showed integrity?

For enrichment, try these ideas:

★ Engage students in making posters, illustrating moments when Ping showed integrity. For extension, have them also draw ways in which he showed great accountability in problem-solving.

★ Challenge students to create a class integrity or honesty pledge.

★ Help students create a bibliography showcasing books that remind them about integrity.

★ Have students author their own storybook about a time it was difficult to be honest and show integrity.

★ Ask students to evaluate the importance of sharing a story like *The Empty Pot* with other children their age. Would they recommend that other teachers or parents read this story to elementary-aged students? What about older students? Let them explain their reasoning in a persuasive paragraph.

★ Encourage students to journal the answers to the following questions: Why is it critical that your friends show integrity? How can you tell if a friend has integrity? Would you be able to be friends with someone who isn't honest and doesn't show integrity?

★ If you've got a community partner who might donate some seeds, send a packet home for students to plant to reinforce the tale.

★ Use the story as a springboard for a science lesson on plant growth. Why would a cooked seed not grow? Let students experiment and see for themselves, and then have them chart or map their observations.

After reading the story aloud, why not sing "A Good Friend" to the tune of "Did You Ever See a Lassie?"

> Have you ever had a good friend, a good friend, a good friend?
> Have you ever had a good friend with integrity?
> A good friend is honest and will keep her promise.
> Have you ever had a good friend who's real trustworthy?

Let students write the lyrics to the next verse and see what happens. It'll beautifully set up your discussion about friends that fit. Like friends, shoes come in all shapes and sizes, but for a pair to be a good fit, it has to be the right shape and size for your feet. The best way to get the perfect fit is to try on shoes before you take them home. That's kind of how it works with friends, too. If they're going to be a good fit for you, your friends should have qualities and values that connect and align with you. So what, exactly, do your students look for in a friend? Brainstorm a list and find out. For example, is it important their friends be nice? Pretty? Truthful? Kind? Respectful? Rich? Responsible? Athletic? Smart? Funny? Generous? Fair? What other things might (or might not) make a good fit in a friend? Give students time to discuss and explain their answers. Prepare to be fascinated by what they think and say. Before moving on, have them do a word cloud with the traits that they think make them a good-fit friend.

There are also tricky-fit shoes. You know the ones, they seem to fit you in the store, but when you try them on the next morning, they hurt your feet and don't really fit at all. You may give them a chance, but you quickly find they leave blisters on your feet. This can happen with friends, too. What kinds of things do tricky-fit friends do that cause blisters in a friendship? Lie? Cheat? Steal? Break promises? Spread rumors? Gossip? Hit? Use mean words?

Ask students what they do with tricky-fit shoes. Have the students pair up and share to find out from each other, then ask: What are your strategies for self-care with tricky-fit friends?

One strategy that we use at our school is taking a friendship time-out. We actually use our hands to make a T, signaling that we need a break, that something about the relationship isn't working well right now, and that we need a time-out. The T is a very empowering tool for a student who's stuck in a yo-yo or tricky-fit relationship. What other gestures can students think of that might work? What other options do they have with tricky-fit friends?

Role-play some tricky-fit friend scenarios like these:

★ What would you do if one friend said that you can't be friends with your other friend anymore?

★ What would you say if one friend started saying mean things about your other friends?

★ What might happen if your friend gave you a "best friend" necklace but then wanted it back?

★ What would you do if you saw your best friend take something that wasn't his or hers?

Finally, there are shoes that just don't fit us anymore. Maybe your feet have outgrown them. Maybe they don't give you the support you need anymore. Teach your children that when friends go in a different direction and just don't fit anymore, it's okay to say goodbye and walk away. Since this needs to be done with dignity and respect, we must give students the words that they'll need and practice these conversations with them so that they learn to navigate socially through life as they look for and find friends that fit.

Here are a few of my good-fit friendship favorites:

Big Wolf and Little Wolf by Nadine Brun-Cosme
> What will happen to Big Wolf's heart when Little Wolf disappears?

Duck & Goose by Tad Hills
> Duck and Goose both want what's best for their little "egg," but they get more than they bargain for as they attempt to help it hatch.

Fox Makes Friends by Adam Relf
> What ingredients does Fox need to make a friend?

Milo Armadillo by Jan Fearnley
> Milo isn't exactly what Tallulah was looking for in a friend, but will he do?

Our Friendship Rules by Peggy Moss and Dee Dee Tardiff
> What happens when the new girl comes between two friends?

The New Bear at School by Carrie Weston
> Who'll accept and befriend Boris, the misfit newbie?

The Sandwich Swap by Queen Rania of Jordan Al Abdullah
> PB&J or hummus? Will differences separate these fast friends?

You Can Be a Friend by Tony and Lauren Dungy
> What will happen when Jade wants to invite her wheelchair-bound friend Hannah to her birthday party at the water park?

Follow up with opportunities for your students to use their friendship skills for good. Let the students take turns being the "Class Friend" or "Family Friend" for a day. Write a job description. What would that look like in your classroom? Or at home in your family? What responsibilities would the "Class Friend" or "Family

Friend" have? How would this person positively make a difference? Make a list of dos and don'ts. Or have students draw pictures of this friend in action. Just like a medic carries a first-aid kit, imagine that the "Class Friend" was going to carry a friendship kit. What items would the students put in it? Bandages to heal hurts? A stick of gum because friends stick together? A rubber band because friends are flexible? See what your friends come up with and decide upon. If you can negotiate the list down to twelve items, it'd be easy enough to actually put the kit together, as a visual for that traveling job.

Another book that I use to reinforce the value of honesty is *Ruthie and the (Not So) Teeny, Tiny Lie* by Laura Rankin.

Start the discussion by looking at Ruthie on the front cover. What's she doing? And how is she feeling about it? Ask your students if sneaking or hiding things is ever a good idea. Find out if they know what *little white lies* are. Is there a difference between a *little white lie* and a real lie?

In this clever tale, an adorable young fox named Ruthie, who LOVES teeny, tiny things, finds a cute camera on the playground and claims that it is hers. After all, "finders keepers, losers weepers," right? When she's confronted by Martin, who says he got that camera for his birthday, Ruthie lies so that she can keep the little treasure. But when Ruthie's lie catches up with her, will she do the right thing and tell the truth?

Ruthie imagines a lot of different consequences for her actions. Ask students if they think the teacher should have punished Ruthie for taking the camera. How about for lying about it? Find out from students why the bus ride home was SO long in the middle of the book, but not that long in the end.

After a riveting discussion about the roles of Ruthie, Martin, the teacher, and Ruthie's parents, reinforce the lesson by having your students recite this little poem: *If you mess it up, you need to clean it up.* To add some fun, try saying it in Ruthie's teeny, tiny voice and then in the voices of the other characters in the book. Then try a grandma or grandpa voice, a squeaky mouse voice, a dog or cat voice, or a giant bear voice.

For some meaningful movement, play the theme song to the *Pink Panther* and have kids practice sleuthing around to encourage them to play the role of a detective and be Truth Sleuths. If there were such a job, what would a Truth Sleuth do? Then find out what they think about sneaking around. Is there ever a time when sneaking around is a good thing? When? What about lying? Is there ever a time when not telling the truth is okay? When? How about not keeping your promise? What kind of situation might require breaking a promise?

Want more real-life applications? Try a friendship treasure hunt. Lead with this inquiry: If you were to head out on a treasure hunt looking for items that represent your friendships, what would you bring back? Ask students to pair up and share a list of things that represent the trademarks of a friendship that works. Then compare and contrast their lists with the others in the class. Finally, challenge students to come up with some reasonable connections between a healthy friendship and the items on this list. Ask them what the following treasures have to do with friendship: a maraca, a puppy, a scarf, headphones, a candle, keys, a river rock, a fishing pole, coffee beans, a goldfish net, toothpaste, and a postage stamp. There aren't really any wrong answers to this activity as long as students think it through and can explain their reasoning. The maraca, for example, can represent music because friends live in harmony.

My friend Lisa used to always tell me, "To have a friend, you've got to be a friend." What does that mean to you? Find out if students agree or disagree and let them explain why in a newsroom-style commentary. Or host a debate. Send students digging through your collection of books and see what quotes they can uncover right in your own classroom or school library. Use the quotes they find as discussion starters for class meetings, journaling, or to make a Public Service Announcement campaigning for friendship.

Then enjoy the show as you watch your superheroes soar from understanding and embracing honor to walking the talk, just like Honest Abe.

Chapter 7

E IS FOR ENTHUSIASM

Let's face it; enthusiasm ignites greatness. I saw this claim on a poster once and I totally believe that it's spot on: "A healthy dose of enthusiasm is like passion on steroids." If only we could bottle it, I think we could make a fortune. But it can't be bought or sold. No, enthusiasm is the by-product of a natural high, the endorphins that your brain produces when it's sparked by choices. Superheroes are enthusiastic about what they do because they get to orchestrate how their rescue is going to play itself out. With the adrenaline dump during a fight or flight situation, they've got the ability to leap tall buildings in a single bound. That's crazy energy.

When was the last time you were enthusiastic—genuinely enthusiastic—about something? What ignited that passion? And what was the end result?

The single thing that seems to excite my students about their relationship with me is my delight to be in their presence. I show enthusiasm for them because I love what I do. It sparks my brain to create engaging lessons that will take them through the domains of character and then release them back into the world with a booster shot of enthusiasm to practice and refine their newly learned skills in the behavioral domain.

Here's an example. Bryce was in the first grade when I first read *The Band-Aid Chicken: A Program about Resisting Peer Pressure* by counselor Becky Rengal Henton. Hoping to give each student a bandage as a tangible takeaway, I'd found out that one of our moms was employed by Johnson & Johnson and was so excited that they'd donate the nearly one thousand bandages that I'd need to enrich that particular peace class. As I remember it, the discussions went well and I was so excited to watch as students connected the pecking order of chickens to a real-life playground pecking order. As each student made the promise never to peck, I mean pick, on others, I handed out the Band-Aids® to seal the deal, to represent an emotional bleed on the inside. The day after Bryce got his bandage, his mom saw him wearing it over his heart. Not knowing it came from the lesson, she asked him why he had his shirt off and a bandage on and then fussed at him to quit wasting Band-Aids®. She couldn't believe what came next. She heard Bryce say that he was wearing the Band-Aid® because his brother had said something mean that had hurt his heart. He went on to enthusiastically recount the details of *The Band-Aid Chicken* and how I had given him that bandage to help him deal with inside bleeds. One little bandage and a chicken puppet had sparked an engagingly enthusiastic dose of greatness, and I was energized beyond belief.

But is enthusiasm something we can teach? Or is it more caught than taught? My sense is that all too often we squelch enthusiasm because it can be difficult to contain. But instead of worrying about how to contain it, I propose that we give students permission to get excited and show unbridled enthusiasm, passion, and verve. What have we got to lose? And what if the benefits far outweigh the cost?

We talked a little bit about attitude in the perseverance chapter. Let's revisit it with a fun title about a dog named Sid. *Some Dogs Do* by Jez Alborough is a rhyming story about a young hound dog who discovers a joyful feeling that "filled him up so much he found his paws just lifted off the ground." When he tries to convince his friends that he can fly, nobody will believe him, not even his teacher. Challenged to demonstrate his fanciful flight, Sid is so discouraged that he's unable to get off of the ground. The dejected dog goes home, where he's comforted by his parents. There, Dad lets him in on a secret about attitude and altitude.

Use this tribute to the power of positive thinking to talk with your students about attitude.

★ What exactly is attitude?

★ Where does attitude come from?

★ Who controls attitude for us?

★ Find out if your students agree with the adage "Your attitude determines your altitude."

★ How does that saying relate to what Sid experienced in the story?

After you've discussed the story, download and dance to the song "Dalmatian Disco" by Captain Music to add meaningful movement to this high-flying tale.

Sing "Who Controls Your Attitude?" to the tune of "Do Your Ears Hang Low?"

Who controls your attitude when you're in a happy mood?
Are you wearing a big smile, will you go that extra mile?
Sharing joy with everyone helps you shine just like the sun.
I control my attitude.
Who controls your attitude when you're in a grumpy mood?
Do you find you're acting rude? Are you whiney? Do you brood?
Don't get angry, scream, or pout; exercise and work it out.
I control my attitude.
Who controls your attitude when you're in a thankful mood?

Are you showing gratitude for good friends and healthy food?
And for sunshine and for rain, for your body and your brain?
I control my attitude.
Who controls your attitude when you're in a tearful mood?
Do you feel so very blue? Are you sad and lonely, too?
Share your feelings with a friend and the sadness soon will end.
I control my attitude.

Now let your students write the next verse!

Enthusiasm is all about attitude. We must teach our superheroes first and foremost by modeling true passion and spark for our jobs, our hobbies, our relationships, and our lives. If we approach every day as another opportunity rather than just another chore, positivity is in our corner and we're sure to feel the joy that comes with intentionally looking for and purposefully seeking out the sunny side of life.

Search for a definition of enthusiasm and the first one to come up sums it up best: "intense and eager enjoyment, interest or approval."

Who wouldn't want feelings of intense and eager enjoyment?

Think about the enthusiasm that the book *Elf on a Shelf: A Christmas Tradition* by Carol V. Aebersold and her daughter, Chandra Bell, has generated since its debut in 2005. Out-of-control mayhem that spread like wildfire. One little story that took over the holiday market like gangbusters. Teachers sending home Elf journals because the student buzz about what their elves were up to was interfering with instruction. Parents and guardians were at home concocting creative shenanigans like elves who were found lying on the laundry room floor in washing detergent that's been made to look like the snow that they've supposedly made their snow angels in. How does this happen?

Enthusiasm is contagious. One little spark can put a little pep into someone's step and before you know it, voilà, everyone is walking a little taller, a little lighter, and a little bit happier. One small idea. One tiny seed. One little elf. It's the Tickle Me Elmo, the Barbie Doll, the Tinker Toys, the Lincoln Logs. Wisdom from an old campfire song: "It only takes a spark to get a fire going." And so it goes, that enthusiasm ignites greatness. An enthusiastic visionary writes the Christmas-themed story that explains how Santa knows who's naughty and nice and almost a decade and more than six million copies later, it's still going strong. If we can engage and enthuse that many readers with one self-published bestseller, imagine what we ought to be able to do in our classrooms when we create lessons that we're passionate about. In his book *Teach Like a PIRATE: Increase Student Engagement, Boost Your Creativity, and Transform Your Life as an Educator,* author Dave Burgess wonders aloud if we have lessons that people would be willing to buy tickets to attend.[21] Hmmm.

Music is also a great motivator that can positively enhance your mood, strengthen weakened emotions, and jump-start your enthusiasm. Do you have a theme song? I adopted the Rose Falcon pop hit "Up, Up, Up" as mine. Not only does it have an incredibly joyful beat, but it's also got lemons-into-lemonade lyrics that inspire and enthuse me. There's nothing I can't do while I'm deeply entrenched in that song. Download it and see for yourself. There's powerful potential and positivity in lyrics. Ask your students to pick a theme song or choose one as your class song. "Home" by Phillip Phillips would be an excellent choice.

The people you surround yourself with make a difference as well. According to Joyce Landorf Heatherly's *Balcony People,*[22] those people in life who energize others and cheer them on are part of an elite group called balcony people. Who are the "balcony people" in a superhero's life? And what's their secret? Happiness is a choice, but there are some useful strategies that can feed that enthusiasm. People who spend time on their balconies get plenty of sunshine for their daily doses of vitamin D; it's a huge part of the reason for their contentedness. According to our friends at the Sunshine Vitamin website[23] humans spend less time in the sun today than at any point in human history, which is why more than one billion people worldwide are vitamin D deficient. Sunshine not only helps your mood, but as little as fifteen to twenty minutes of sun twice a week can make a positive difference in your health. Water also affects mood. The Agricultural Research Service[24] recently found that dehydration is associated with negative mood, including fatigue and confusion, so "water" you waiting for? Make a pact to stay hydrated and see how good it feels as your mood elevates.

Showing appreciation can also help your attitude. Why not keep a "Blessings Book" to help you cultivate an attitude of gratitude. Or make it a "Joy Journal." Find something to write about every day and make time for your students to do the same. Carry blank thank-you cards with you so that you can follow up acts of kindness with a note of thanks or affirmation. Acts of kindness, both planned and random, also result in significant physical and mental health benefits. It just feels good to appreciate and be appreciated.

What are you enthusiastic about and whom have you motivated lately? Your motivator can be something as simple as a smile. In the story *One Voice* by Cindy McKinley, a young boy's kind act affects more than twenty stakeholders and ignites enthusiasm and ultimately provides a day-maker for each of them. How else can you motivate? Catch students doing good things and affirm them for their excellent choices.

Reflect on your favorite inspirational quotes or search online for some that grab your attention and make you think. Use those quotes to make mini-posters. Let students choose one of these or their favorite, and then have them illustrate it with an inspirational picture.

Can there possibly be power in something as simple as positive thinking?

Research says yes, there is. But, according to Zig Ziglar, motivation has to be part of your intentional daily routine: "People always say that motivation doesn't last. Well, neither does bathing. That's why we recommend it daily."[25]

Any (or all) of these ideas would be an excellent way to muster up the motivation you need and put your enthusiasm to work and ignite greatness.

Chapter 8

R IS FOR RESPONSIBILITY

As farmers, we gained a huge capacity for responsibility because opportunities to respond on a farm abound. Out of necessity, we learned to risk mitigate, trouble-shoot, and problem-solve. When the frozen-tundra winds blew snow everywhere, for example, we instinctively set our alarm clocks to awaken a bit earlier because we knew we'd have to dig our way into the barns and quite possibly unfreeze pipes before our duties could begin. My father learned all sorts of skills because his chores included those of a veterinarian, a mechanic, an agronomist, and a businessman. We bred our own cattle and helped birth the calves whose moms were struggling during delivery. We fixed tractors as they broke down so we could till, fertilize, plow, and plant the fields. We paid our bills with the money that the milk brought in, and we borrowed money when we couldn't make ends meet. We sharpened our ability to respond to any situation that might come our way. In a way, farmers have to be superheroes.

I love to ask students what chores they have. Sometimes they tell me a whole laundry list, other times they tell me they don't have any. I feel bad for kids who don't have chores. I always let them know that I consider homework a chore and that it's important that we take our chores seriously. One way to visually show this is by using a Chore Chain. Give each student a slip of paper to write a list of their chores. The younger learners can draw a picture of their chores; maybe they feed the puppy, so they can draw a dog or a dog-food bowl. After they've finished their slips, have them share their chores aloud for all to hear. Staple them together to make a Chore Chain. Show students the completed chain and talk about how all of the links of a chain make it longer and add strength. Then select a link somewhere in the middle, read it aloud, and tell the class that this student didn't get his/her chores done. This tears the link and breaks the chain in two. The chain might still work, but it's been weakened because it's been compromised. Talk about what we'd need to do to restore its strength. Tear it a few more times and let the links fall to the ground to show what'll happen as the consequences of our choices catch up with us.

Another fun idea is to play Chore Bingo. Make a 5 x 5 grid using the word CHORE across the top. Let the middle square be a NO HOMEWORK free space. Brainstorm with the class a list of thirty (or more!) chores that children their age could do. Then let students select the twenty-four chores from the list that they have done or think they could do and write those onto the blank cards you've given them. While they're completing their cards, you write all of the chores from their list and cut them in strips that you can choose from a cup or pile to call in the Chore Bingo game. If the chore you call matches one that your student has written or drawn in, he/she covers it up with a token, a chip, or a penny. If they get five in a row or four corners and the middle, they've got a BINGO. Maybe the winners could earn a free homework pass or five minutes of extra recess for the class.

When I teach tomorrow's leaders about responsibility, they learn that it's all about choices, consequences, chores, and stakeholders. On a farm, we didn't really have a lot of choices about our chores necessarily, but had we chosen to not show up and milk the cows, the natural consequences could be devastating to the animals. But who are the other stakeholders? A stakeholder is someone who's involved in your choices, someone who has a stake in your life, someone who cares. Simply put, a stakeholder is anyone who is involved, whom your choice might affect. So say we decide to take a few days off from milking without getting our chores covered.

Who are the stakeholders? The cows that could very easily get sick. The veterinarian we'd have to call. The dairy that's expecting a certain amount of milk per our contract. The customers who won't get their milk, cheese, butter, or ice cream. Who else might be involved?

It's never too early to start talking with your students about stakeholders. It always surprises them how many people can be involved and have a stake in their every choice. I'll routinely start a peace class lesson with a problem poster and ask them to identify the stakeholders. Then I marvel that it'll come up at lunch when I'm dining with small groups of students in the Counselor Café; students will be telling me a story, then say something like, "That's a lot of stakeholders, isn't it, Mrs. Gruener?" Score!

Try this sticky situation: A child put some glue in another student's hair. Ask students to name the stakeholders and explain how they are involved. Expect answers like: both students, their parents or guardians, the teacher, the principal, the counselor, the nurse. Why the nurse? In case there's an allergic reaction, right? A hair stylist. Who else is involved? The glue company? A lawyer? As you talk with them about a worst-case scenario, let them stand up to represent the stakeholders and watch what happens. Before you know it, they'll all be standing and it'll serve as a great visual to help them understand stakeholders.

Or use one of these scenarios: You forget your puppy on the porch overnight. Your friend's family adopts a baby. The pitcher on your team is late for your baseball game. Your school counselor is severely injured in a head-on collision one day after school.

Try this ditty as an echo poem or sing it to the tune of "Frère Jacques":

What's responsibility? Staying in control of me.
Doing my chores faithfully. Making choices carefully.
Thinking 'bout the stakeholders. Thinking 'bout the consequences.
You can count on me. Responsibility.

And what kind of literature can you use to connect these concepts with fictional or real characters? I was so excited to find the book *Squawking Matilda* by Lisa Horstman because it's got **responsibility** written all over it—responsibility to projects, responsibility to promises, and responsibility to pets.

This book is about best effort. It also has a caring and compassion component that might just pull at your heartstrings a bit. Like a lot of little ones, Mae has a ton of creative ideas, some of which work out, some of which do not. She also tends, like a lot of us, to get distracted easily and fly from one project to the next, sometimes without completing either one. So when Matilda comes along, caring for a chicken seems like a worthwhile cause, but Mae gets distracted and Matilda feels forgotten. What will it take to find Matilda when she goes missing to reconnect with that scrappy bird? And can Mae ultimately win Matilda over and secure her happiness?

Responsibility is a huge word with even bigger significance.

★ Who are the stakeholders in Mae's story?

★ What are some things that Mae does in the story that don't quite work out?

★ What does Mae do that does work out well?

★ Is Mae a good problem solver? How do you know?

★ Is Mae good at taking responsibility? At showing responsibility?

★ Are those two things the same or different?

★ How did Mae show responsibility toward her projects?

★ How did she show responsibility toward her promise to Aunt Susan?

★ How did she show responsibility toward Matilda?

★ What was that experience like for them?

★ And what, if anything, does this story have to do with the state-mandated assessments that are just around the corner for many of us?

Want to infuse some meaningful movement? Break out the "Chicken Dance" music after you see what happens to make this proud chicken Mae's "best project yet!" Then sing this little ditty to the Mickey Mouse Club theme song with your chore champs:

When I do things to the best of my ability, I'm
R-E-S P-O-N S-I-B-L-E!
I think before I act so that my friends can count on me, because I'm
R-E-S P-O-N S-I-B-L-E!
Do what's right (clap, clap, clap), day and night (clap, clap, clap).
Always take responsibility (two, three, four)
Do what I'm supposed to do, stay in control of me. It shows I'm
R-E-S P-O-N S-I-B-L-E!

Once students understand and embrace the idea of responsibility, it's time to give them opportunities to behave responsibly. What chores or jobs do your students have? In school? At home? In their group or club? With their friends? It's so hard for grown-ups like me to give up our control. I grew up in a home where a frustrated mom often threw up her hands with exhaustion and shouted, "Never mind, I'll do it myself!" So guess what I did when my own children were in their formative years? Then I heard a wise counselor, Ginger Robinson, speak at a counselors' conference and what she said some fifteen years ago has stuck like glue: We must never, ever yell at a child. My first thought was, "What? Is she serious?" And my very next thought was, "Oops, too late." When we shout at our children, guess what they learn? And when we swoop in and rescue them from failure or save them from tasks or responsibilities, guess what we teach them? So put away those reins and let go. It'll be hard, but you can do it. Responsibility isn't about being perfect; it's about pursuing excellence with your best effort. Just best effort, that's it. Resist the urge to move them over to take over. No one will learn anything that way, except dependence, that they need you to do tasks that they could. Don't just tell your superheroes that they can, show them by letting them show you. Let them be responsible so that they can be responsible. It was providential that I heard Ginger speak that day because I realized that it's never too late to do a better job. Let your superheroes take age-appropriate tasks, chores, and responsibilities and watch them become independent thinkers and learners.

Every day at Westwood-Bales, we recite a character pledge that our leadership team wrote: *I will make good choices today. I will respect myself, my teachers, and others, and give my best effort in all I do.* It's our promise to ourselves and each other and serves as a springboard for reflection and correction when we do stumble along the way. Superheroes possess a keen ability to respond because they make sure they're in the right place at the right time, doing what they can to right wrongs.

Chapter 9

O IS FOR OBEDIENCE

If only I had ten cents for every time my parents told us to "obey your elders." I had a bus driver named Elder, so literal, kindergarten me really took that to heart en route to and from school. Over time, I learned to extend that obedience from our elders, who were wise and knew better, to obeying all rules and laws. Why? I used to think it was my parents hoping that their children would positively reflect the values that they stood for and had worked diligently to teach. I had what I thought might be evidence of that when my father would tell me that he didn't want any gifts for his birthday or Christmas, just good kids. Obedient kids. And quickly it became clear that obeying laws and rules wasn't just a good idea, but it really was the safest practice. "Be careful with those scissors," "Don't run in the hallways," and "Watch out" were commonplace and all meant to remind us to follow directions and be safe. Without rules, after all, we risk danger and chaos.

At the University of Wisconsin, I took a philosophy course and learned about Immanuel Kant and free will. The lecture on whether or not walking on the grass is inherently wrong is as clear to me as if it had happened yesterday. Does your answer to that change if there is a sign posted telling you to keep off the grass? How is it different if it's posted as a request that reads: "Please help our grass grow"? It made me wonder who decides what's right and wrong, and it forever put me on the sidewalk.

Two picture books that tackle the universality laws based on Kant's categorical imperative are *If Everybody Did* by Jo Ann Stoval and *What If Everybody Did That?* by Ellen Javernick. Basically both books address the cause and effect of the free-for-all that would result from not obeying the rules and laws set in place. What would happen if people didn't follow the rules, just one time?

Apply the questions to school: What would happen if everybody left their dirty cafeteria trays on the table? What would happen if everybody arrived late? What if nobody flushed the toilet? What if everybody ran in the halls? What if nobody waited his/her turn at the water fountain?

When applied at home: What if nobody mowed the lawn? What if nobody did the laundry? What if nobody fed the pets? Or what if nobody washed the dishes? What if nobody went grocery shopping?

Apply the question to the community and beyond: What would happen if nobody obeyed the speed limit? What if everybody threw trash out the car windows? What if nobody obeyed the leash law? What if everybody shoplifted?

After discussing or writing about these "if...then" scenarios, ponder with your students what would happen if everybody did the right thing. What would their world be like at home if everybody did their chores? What would school be like if everybody followed the rules and treated one another with respect? What would their community, and beyond, be like if everybody obeyed the laws and was a good citizen?

Superheroes spring into action when somebody's causing chaos by not following the rules. Good citizens obey rules and make wherever they go better because they're there. Find out from your little superheroes how their school family is better because they're a part of it. How is their classroom better? How is her physical education class better because she's a teammate? How is the choir better because he sings along? How is the chess club better?

Not only do good citizens obey laws and rules, but they also vote, serve, and conserve. While there is no rule that we must recycle, for example, it's a promising practice because it gives us a chance to reuse and repurpose the things that we can, in an attempt to conserve what resources we have. Good citizens are also good neighbors and they respect and protect the environment. Good citizens show good sportsmanship. They play by the rules and they don't find it necessary to argue with or boo the other team or the umpires or referees. Consider this dilemma: A wide receiver on the football team catches a pass, avoids a tackle, and heads toward the end zone for a touchdown. In the process, however, he lost his helmet so a flag was thrown, the touchdown was negated by the penalty, and the play was resumed at the point at which his helmet had come off. That's when the crowd started to boo. Were they booing the referees or the rules? Does it matter? The rules, put in place to help ensure the safety of the player, don't allow for a player to continue play without a helmet, so that receiver was actually ineligible to advance the ball once his helmet was off. Would a good citizen boo? Why or why not? Sometimes the answers to these dilemmas aren't crystal clear. Maybe the crowd doesn't know the rule that brought that ball back. Does that matter? Challenge your super-citizens with food for thought like this. Examples abound in the newspaper and online every day. I'll never forget this teen named Tommy.

Cross-country running is about staying the course. It can be kind of lonely and it may seem a lot longer than the three miles you know it to be. The course isn't typically smooth by any means, and it's often riddled with challenges like hills, holes, bends, and brush. A bit like life, really. Imagine now that you're the kind of kid who isn't really a natural runner, who doesn't necessarily even like running, much less competing. The kind of kid who's giving it his all but whose all doesn't seem to be nearly enough. Ever. Maybe the kind of kid whose inner voice is talking him out of even finishing the trail. Maybe he needs the team more than the team needs him. What would you want? What would you need?

That's where Tommy comes in. A high school senior, Tommy doesn't know this kid. In fact, Tommy, a runner for an opposing team, is actually just a spectator during this particular race. I'm not sure if he has already run his race or if he's about to, and I'm not sure if it really matters. What matters is that when Tommy notices this kid and sees that he's struggling, he joins the crowd in encouraging him and cheering him on. And then Tommy does something that no one else does. He jumps into the race to pace the kid. To whisper words of encouragement and talk him through his breathing, keeping him in the game mentally and physically. Not just with words but with actions, by running the course. Tommy saw a need, listened to his heart, and helped that kid, who was clearly running on empty, finish the race. This kid he's never even met.

Touched by Tommy's compassion and sportsmanship, that kid's coach wrote a note of affirmation and thanks to Tommy's coach. The coach read that letter at the cross-country banquet, and Tommy got a standing ovation, not for being the Most Valuable Player, not for winning the most medals or for making it to State, but for his strength of character. When good goes, it always comes back around. It reassures me to know that there are teens like Tommy in this world, ready to help pace me next time I'm running on empty.

If you need more examples of this, search online for the sports story called "Touching Them All" in which a Western Oregon softball player hurts herself rounding the bases on her first and only home run hit. When the rules prohibited her teammates from touching her, players on the opposing Central Washington team asked permission to carry her across home plate. Or "A Game of Hope," the story of a coach in Grapevine, Texas, who sent out a letter to his team parents asking them to sit on the opposing team's side and cheer for their players since they were inmates and wouldn't have fans of their own. These two clips show sportsmanship at its finest, orchestrated by athletes who looked outside of themselves and saw needs that trumped their own glory.

What's the difference between sportsmanship and gamesmanship? Being coached to run up a score, for example, or to hurt someone to get them out of the game. Some people don't see anything wrong with certain practices like this, but in Texas a football team was actually accused of bullying when they won 91 to 0. What do your caped crusaders think about this?

Consider the expression "There's an exception to every rule." So what happens if two rules collide? And how does a superhero decide if a rule is unjust? Does fair necessarily mean equal? And is there a way to peacefully protest something that doesn't seem fair? I instantly think about Anne Frank or Rosa Parks, but again, examples abound if you'll only spark awareness in your students' hearts and minds and teach them to discern between right and wrong. Explore with them an inquiry like this: Does a superhero **always** obey? Or can they posit examples of when a superhero might not be able to abide by the rules? Talk about the effectiveness of a zero-tolerance policy. Is it right that someone who defends himself or herself can also be in trouble? Again, a little muddy, isn't it? But that's okay, because superheroes don't shy away from courageous conversations and conflict resolution.

To give students ownership and increase efficacy among class families, we work together to create our promises to one another instead of just posting a set of rules that the teacher and students follow. This has served us well because it becomes a working document that students can use to hold one another accountable and encourage each other to "check yourself" if there's an issue in conflict with the class contract.

Finally, seal the deal with a little "Gotta Be Fair" ditty using the hand-jive motions for a bonus movement opportunity:

    ♪ *Gotta be fair, you've gotta be fair.*
You gotta take turns, and you've got to share!
You've gotta be fair, just gotta be fair.
Gotta obey the rules, all the time and everywhere.

Challenge students to revise my poem or write a second verse of their own.

Students can only obey rules insofar as they know what they are. To level the playing field and make situations equitable, good citizens know the rules up front, before the games begin. Rules are in place to keep us safe and keep things fair. Good citizens cannot be at peace with a world of confusion and chaos; they obey laws and follow rules so that the world can be an orderly, peaceful place to live.

Chapter 10

E IS FOR ENCOURAGEMENT

Ah, the gift of encouragement. It's all about giving someone approval, support, confidence, and hope. Superheroes encourage by example when they courageously come to the rescue to restore hope. But is it inherited or learned? I think it's a little bit of both. Let's look at the word and its subsequent skill set a bit more closely. The root word in encouragement is courage, the ability to do something that frightens you, strength in the face of pain or grief.

Superheroes are known for their unwavering courage and bravery, but before we can encourage one another, a healthy awareness about courage is a must. So we talk about being brave. A lot. Try asking students what scares them, frightens them, or makes them feel afraid. They know. Make a list of the things that cause them fear before finding out what strategies they have to combat fear and uncover courage. One of my favorite tools to teach about courage is the book *Some Things Are Scary* by Florence Parry Heide. This isn't a story, but a list of things that the narrator finds scary. As you read, students will have fun parroting the "is scary!" pattern, "Watching your best friend move away…is scary." Some of the pages will hit close to home and be VERY real while others will be a ridiculous exaggeration and prompt laughs. Stop at each page and find out from your courageous kids which of the scenarios or situations with which they connect the most.

Fear underlies a lot of out-of-control or undesirable behaviors in children who might not yet have the vocabulary and maturity to express verbally how they're feeling. Talking with students about their anxieties and brainstorming ways to manage their fears can be very empowering. See if they connect with placing their fears into a worry box, drawing out their worries, making friends with their worries, or using a worry rock as a touchstone. Find out what or who helps your students be brave when they feel frightened. I find the "then what?" technique helpful when I'm trying to dig deeper and figure out what's at the base of behaviors. Think about the child who is acting out because he's changing modes of transportation and he's worried that his mom won't be there to pick him up after school.

Teacher/Parent: "I can tell that you're worried about your change in transportation plans."
Child: "Yes."
Teacher/Parent: "Okay, let's say your mom's not there. Then what?"
Child: "Well, then I won't get picked up."
Teacher/Parent: "Then what?"
Child: "I'll have to stay at school."
Teacher/Parent: "Then is there someone else we could call?"
Child: "Yes, we can call Grandma."
Teacher/Parent: "Then what?"
Child: "She'll come get me. But what if Mom didn't come and get me because she's hurt?"

Might seem like a stretch, but remember those courageous conversations that we talked about in the previous chapter? Sometimes it takes a little more digging, but it's worth mining the worries for more deeply seated fears so that we can combat them more effectively. Other books about courage that students could use to compare and contrast with a double-bubble graphic organizer are *Courage* by Bernard Faber, *Scaredy Squirrel* by Mélanie Watt, *You've Got Dragons* by Kathryn Cave, *What Was I Scared of?* by Dr. Seuss, *Is a Worry Worrying You?* by Ferida Wolff, *Don't Worry Bear* by Greg Foley, *Wemberly Worried* by Kevin Henkes, and *Go Away Worries!* by Michelle White.

As a follow-up activity, students can make a two-door foldable. On the left, it can say and show, "I used to be afraid of _____." On the right, it can say and show, "But then I tried _____." On the inside, it can say and show, "Now I am courageous!"

Besides modeling courage by being brave in the face of fears, how else can we encourage one another? One of my favorite ways to encourage is the "Day Maker" phone call. We know that what we encourage, we teach, so when I see a behavior that we'd like more of, I call home to affirm and to encourage. Sometimes I have to leave a message. Sometimes I actually get to talk to a mom, dad, or guardian. Either way, I let them know how proud we are of his/her child's choices or that it's clear that he/she is doing something right. I finish by encouraging the person on the other end of the line to keep up the hard work! I'll do this in the drop-off line, too, when a child gets out of the car with a greeting, a compliment, or a smile. It's a win-win because I feel just as good noticing as the family member does getting noticed.

Sometimes encouragement comes packaged in the written word. Look around for good things to happen. Then write students and/or their parents a note about what you experienced. Carry sticky notes with you in the hallways and post notes of encouragement onto quality work hanging on bulletin boards. Write an email sharing with the family your pride about who they are and what they are doing to make their classroom and your school a better place. My favorite gifts over the years have been handwritten notes of thanks, caring, and love. Students draw me pictures of rainbows, peace signs, and happiness. During my recovery from the head-on car collision that very easily could have taken my life, school family members wrote me cards of healing and hope. One that will forever stay with me simply said, "Kindness doesn't grow on trees; that's why we need you to hurry back." A dash of encouragement is truly worth a pound of cure.

Encouragement can also be sent via pictures. Have students carry around a character camera to catch one another making good choices, learning, growing, exploring, sharing, and leading. Then post them online on your school's website.

Students encourage one another in class circles with good news, bad news, happy news, sad news. Sharing a glimpse into our personal lives connects students to their teacher as well as to each other. Faculty and staff encourage one another by sharing good news and affirmations in faculty gatherings. We've also got an online conference room through our email server where we can publicly affirm one another. It feels good to notice and to be noticed, to affirm and to be affirmed.

We've encouraged attendance weekly by crowning a prompt prince or princess, randomly drawn from the names of everyone who didn't miss any school and arrived on time that week. The prompt prince or princess wears a special crown and gets to use the Principal's Chair as his/her throne for the day. Sometimes we encourage with tangible incentives, like our partnership with the Houston Astros, who give a family a four-pack of tickets to a baseball game for those students with perfect attendance in the third quarter; other times we use less-concrete incentives like "Storytime with Administrators" or a bonus outing to our local nature center. Our parents are also encouraged to take an active role in their child's education. A favorite way we do that is by engaging them in parent homework reflection sheets. Our best assignments have asked, "How does your child color the world with character?" and "What is your child's superpower?" For both of those, the response was overwhelming and the answers each more heartwarming than the next. Parents wrote in and drew pictures of how their children live out our school values. Imagine seeing your parents' words of encouragement hanging on a bulletin board in your school. "Jaxson's superpower is compassion." "Eva colors the world with character by helping others." "Gracie colors the world with character with her generosity." "Zachary's superpower is kindness." A simply powerful encouragement strategy.

First grade teacher Jennifer Quigley is the queen of encouragement in our corner of the world. From the time she meets her class family, she lets them know that they are can-doers. She tells them they can. She shows them that they can. And if they can't yet, she instills hope and confidence by empowering them with the positive message that they can. Then she lets them show her that they can. Friendswood High School graduates come back to Mrs. Quigley year after year to thank her for believing in them and empowering them to believe in themselves. Mrs. Quigley's can-doers never forget that they are can-doers because she brings out the best in her future leaders.

We complete many of our service projects strictly to encourage. We've written get-well cards to take to our local pharmacy, to support and encourage. We sing for veterans at a special program of celebration and thanks, to support and encourage. We've put our character message on pizza boxes to be delivered out in the community, to support and encourage. After units on community workers, we've delivered treats and notes to express our gratitude to local police officers, firemen, post office employees, a nursing home staff member, the Chamber of Commerce, and volunteers at City Hall. We host an annual Grandparents' Day to honor our character role models. And the lesson? Superheroes learn by doing, so they learn to encourage. We've taken it from feeling courage, knowing encouragement, embracing it, and ultimately practicing encouragement.

American author Robert Collier once said, "Many of us, swimming against the tides of trouble the world knows nothing about, need only a bit of praise or encouragement and we will make the goal."[26] French poet and journalist Anatole France claims that, "Nine tenths of education is encouragement."[27] And former chairperson and CEO of the Xerox Corporation Anne M. Mulcahey remarked, "Employees are a company's greatest asset—they're your competitive advantage. You want to attract and retain the best; provide them with encouragement, stimulus, and make them feel they are an integral part of the company's mission."[28] Ultimately, we are preparing our superheroes for the workforce and we must arm them with the skill of encouragement in their arsenal.

Chapter 11

S IS FOR SELF-DISCIPLINE

Life on the farm taught us self-discipline at a very early age. I was milking cows by the age of five and driving a tractor with an attached manure spreader before I was twelve. We learned it out of necessity, really, because my two siblings and I were the "hired" hands. Chores needed to be done before school and again afterward, and we were it. Since the cows didn't take a vacation, we were always on duty. In the milking parlor, self-discipline meant that we got our jobs done without being told what to do. We were self-reliant and could get the tasks done all by ourselves.

In the classroom, self-discipline also includes self-control, a skill with which a younger me sometimes struggled. I remember one specific instance as if it were yesterday. I was in fifth grade and my brother, Tim, was in sixth. Since there were eleven children in each of the two grade levels, both grades were in the same room with the same teacher. I often listened in on what the sixth graders were doing. On this particular day, they were doing Current Events, something I loved. When it came to the bonus question, it tickled me that I knew the answer and none of the students in Tim's grade did. When the teacher said aloud that the answer was "Henry Aaron," I jumped out of my seat to correct her with, "No, it's not! It's Hank, Hank Aaron." Oh, I knew the answer all right, but what I didn't know is that Hank was the nickname for Henry. What happened next wasn't pretty and I quickly learned that showing self-control and being self-disciplined would take me places I'd rather go than out into the hallway to get scolded.

The days of "children are to be seen and not heard" are a thing of the past. Today's young people need to be seen, heard, and understood. They also need to be given permission to try new things and, yes, possibly even fail, so they can learn and grow. Superheroes show self-discipline when they've learned to be resilient and become self-reliant. Fostering self-discipline happens when we turn over control and give our students leadership roles and opportunities along with voice and choice.

According to Conscious Discipline: 7 Basic Skills for Brain Smart Classroom Management by Becky Bailey, research indicates that the brain acts differently when choice is offered. Choice changes the brain's chemistry. When we feel we are lacking in choices, the brain produces norepinephrine, the fight or flight chemical. As a stress hormone, norepinephrine affects parts of the brain where attention and responding actions are controlled. In this state, motivation and morale are low and learning efficiency is poor. Choice can trigger the release of the brain's optimal thinking chemicals, known as endorphins. Endorphins, likened unto natural morphine, increase motivation, reduce stress, create positive feelings, and foster an optimistic "I can" attitude. In short, the child experiences less pain and a general sense of well-being and confidence, empowered even.[29] Who wouldn't want that in a superhero?

Every day, we get to make choices and those choices have consequences, positive and negative. A teacher's task from when kids take that first step into their room is to teach and then empower them in such a way that we could work ourselves out of a job. If we want to nurture independence so that our little learners will soar when they leave our nest, then we have to give them opportunities and permission to practice those skills under our guidance and learn to complete tasks all by themselves.

Try singing this song with them to the tune of "London Bridge Is Falling Down":

I can do things by myself, by myself, by myself.
I can do things by myself; I have discipline.
I'll call you if I need help, I need help, I need help.
I'll call you if I need help; please support me.
When I show self-discipline, discipline, discipline.
When I show self-discipline, it feels awesome!

One of our favorite character assemblies over the years has been the Primary Focus musical called Choices Count. Primary Focus was a group of college-aged singers and dancers who'd committed the year to traveling the country and carrying the character torch. That organization recently dissolved, but their message still resonates with me and my school family. I can still hear these words from their catchy song that encapsulates self-discipline "If It Is To Be, It Is Up To Me".

Teaching students this and then making it happen is not an easy charge. But it's so crucial because every time we rescue a child and let him/her off the hook, so to speak, they've missed an opportunity for growth. And it's not those times from which students learn the self-discipline that would give them wings and take them into the future. It is the times when we don't swoop in to save them that they learn to be self-reliant. Do you know the parable about the woman who helps a struggling butterfly get out of its cocoon but, by doing so, ends up doing it more harm than good? Turns out that the butterfly's wings need that workout to get out from inside the comforts of its natural shell in order for it to emerge strong. Because the lady did the work for the butterfly, the creature didn't complete the chores it inherently needed to do to be successful in life. Essentially, she destined it to die.

Responsibilities and chores are a must for children as they learn to fly from very early on. Children must know from their first day of school that they are valuable members of a class family and that their contributions, no matter the size, make a difference. They'll learn best by doing and then enjoy experiencing the fruits of their labor. Classrooms in which teachers teach concepts and then take the role of the coach and/or facilitator and allow children some ownership and control in their learning turn out self-disciplined, independent children. Why? Because they've given them the knowledge they need followed by an opportunity to apply it, make decisions, stumble, fall down, and get back up again. When teachers train, then turn over the reins, beautiful things happen. Not always right away, but over time. When children are disciplined with dignity and respect, those two traits go with them and they'll follow suit. Superheroes learn self-discipline from being properly trained.

When students are challenged to be self-disciplined, they become problem solvers, decision makers, and critical thinkers. That's because they are not just given answers to remember but they are given decisions to make. When I teach decision making, we talk through four steps: Stop, Look, Think, Decide.

★ Stop: We always benefit from a little bit of time before we jump head first into a decision. Teach children to stop for a moment to give themselves a little thinking time.

★ Look: Look at all of your options. Decisions come with possibilities. Make sure to carefully look at the pros and cons, benefits and burdens of what you're about to decide.

★ Think: Think about possible consequences, both good and bad. Who are the stakeholders and how might your decision affect them? Think about the best possible outcome for everyone involved.

★ Decide: After you've gone through the three steps, you're ready to make that decision. Do so with confidence.

Self-disciplined superheroes also exhibit healthy habits of self-reliance and control. There are physical ways to show self-discipline: eat healthy foods, drink plenty of water, make exercise a routine, get at least eight hours of sleep each night, practice self-care habits like meditation or yoga. There are also emotional ways to exercise self-control: deep-breathing relaxation techniques, anger-management exercises, journaling or drawing out feelings, dialoguing with confidants or counselors.

Being self-disciplined is often about doing what needs to be done even when you don't feel like doing it. It's about prioritizing so work comes first, then play. It's about surrounding yourself with self-disciplined people. Our children must know that every day they get a clean slate on which to write their own stories. They get to figure out what it's going to say. All by themselves, with our guidance, support, and encouragement.

Conclusion

Putting It All Together

As you set up your classrooms, always keep in mind that visibility is an important element of a climate of character. The messages that surround students can't help but influence them. Here are some of the ideas that we've incorporated at our School of Character.

Bulletin Boards

What's hanging on the walls in your character building? In addition to posting student work, we intentionally weave our character mission into our visual displays. Here are some of our favorites:

~ How Do You Make Footsteps Worth Following?
~ We Are All Different but We All Swim in the Same School.
~ Summer Sizzles at Character Camp!
~ My Stars—What Makes You Shine?
~ Welcome to Our Character Dynasty—We're Happy, Happy, Happy You're Here!
~ The Golden Rule Adds Value to Our Character Building.
~ Character Is the True National Treasure.
~ What's Cooking in Your Character Café?
~ Take Note: iTune into Healthy Habits!—How Do You Plug in?
~ CharACTer Is Our Superpower.

~ How Do You Sprinkle Kindness?
~ The Giving Tree: Take What You Need; Give What You Can.
~ "PAWS" for Good Character.
~ How Many Smiles Does It Take to Fill a Bucket?
~ We Swim with the Character Current in Our School.
~ Peace—There's an App for That.
~ Peacemakers Walk the Talk.
~ Every Day Is a Gift—That's Why We Call It the Present.
~ Fruitful Behaviors Stem from Core Values.
~ Kindness Is the Real Global Warming.

From Crayons to College (C2C)—Cultivating What Students Need to Be Ready

My daughter and I created this list campaign as she journeyed through the college-application process. It is by no means exhaustive; what quality ingredients would you include in your recipe for college readiness? While it began as a bulletin board, we also used it as an awareness activity to help students goal set and focus on a skill that they'd like to refine. Share the list with them and ask them which trait they'd like to work on, for a week or a month, maybe even a year. Let them decide. Encourage them to share it with their parents because sometimes saying it out loud and sharing it helps to hold us accountable. Lynette, a blog reader in Utah, turned her C2C campaign into a school-wide incentive. Students were recognized for putting these traits into action, then in a random drawing, one name a month was drawn and that student was named the ambassador for that value and given a $10.00 bill to open or add to their bank account. A local bank then partnered with them and matched that $10.00 deposit for that ambassador.

A – Attitude. Stay positive. "Whether you think you can, or you think you can't, you're right." ~Henry Ford.

B – Behavior. Behave with discipline, wisdom, and self-control.

C – Cooperation. Communicate, collaborate, and cooperate. None of us is as smart as all of us.

D – Determination. Set goals and see them through with tenacity and drive.

E – Effort. Give 100% in everything you do.

F – Family. Let family and friends be there for you. A support system is a valuable asset.

G – Good Grades. Achieve academically. Grade point average (GPA) determines class rank.

H – Honor. Reach for your dreams with dignity and honor.

I – Initiative. Get a jump start on your work. You know what they say about the early bird.

J – Judgment. Use good judgment; it'll help you minimize mistakes and fix them more easily.

K – Knowledge. Take challenging classes. The more you know, the stronger you grow.

L – Leadership. Lead by example. Make tracks worth following.

M – Morals. Let your conscience be your guide, even when nobody's looking.

N – Nutrition. Eat well. A healthy body = a healthy mind.

O – Organization. Get it together. Your stuff won't be helpful if you don't know where it is.

P – Perseverance. Keep going. Persist with your purpose even when there are problems.

Q – Quality. Stamp a quality assurance guarantee on everything you do.

R – Responsibility. Show up on time, make choices carefully, and do what you're supposed to do.

S – Study Skills. Sharpen important navigation tools for school and life by learning how to learn.

T – Time Management. Use a planner. You've got all the time you need when you manage it well.

U – Understanding. Listen, hear, and reflect to understand. Communicate well to be understood.

V – Volunteerism. Lend a helping hand with a servant heart. What goes around, comes around.

W – Work Ethic. Work hard and it'll pay off in ways you can't even imagine.

X – eXcellence. Pursue excellence in everything. It will set you apart.

Y – Yearning. Yearn to learn something new every day. You've got to want it to get it.

Z – Zeal. Race toward your degree (and your career) with all you've got.

Our Character Case

We use our old-fashioned glassed-in display case to highlight and showcase new picture books with a character theme. As students pass by, they're encouraged to talk about which book they'd like to read and why, then make predictions about what happens in that story based on the cover image and its title.

Character Rocks

There are many things that you can do with a two-pound bag of polished river rocks and a marker. Use a fine-tip Sharpie to write the character words from the SUPERHEROES acrostic and their synonyms onto the rocks.

Service—Volunteerism

Unconditional love—Caring

Perseverance—Endurance

Empathy—Understanding

Respect—Manners

Honesty—Trustworthiness

Enthusiasm—Passion

Responsibility—Obligation

Obedience—Duty

Encouragement—Inspiration

Self-Discipline—Self-Control

Then you can try any of the following ideas:

★ Put the rocks on a tray. Have the students study the words. You can discuss them for meaning and have students give examples. Have students close their eyes and then take two or three away. Have students try to remember which ones are gone.

★ Play a game of concentration. Turn the rocks word-side-down and have students flip to find two that belong to the same pillar. For example, honesty and integrity would both go with the trustworthiness pillar, so you'd have a match.

★ Play the antonym game. Either write the opposite on the back of the stone or just discuss what the opposite of each word would be. Or make a second set of stones with opposite words (like dishonesty) and play the concentration game with opposites.

★ Let each student personalize a rock with the trait that he/she wants to work on.

★ Put the rocks into a fountain, planter, or vase as a conversation piece.

Marquee Messages

When we don't have something specific to announce, we'll put positive sayings on the marquee to motivate our community. Here are some of the things we've shared:

~ How will you be a joy maker today?
~ Be cheerful and pass it on.
~ Find yourself in the service of others.
~ Be a Peace Maker.
~ It's All about CAREacter.
~ Character Is Our Anti-Drug.

Actions Speak Louder than Words

All of my words are just that, words, until someone puts them into action just as theories are just theoretical until someone puts them into practice.

What are your students' strengths? If they are not one of the traits in the SUPERHEROES acrostic, then what? The first step in helping your superheroes soar is to identify what makes them fly. The first domain is, after all, the cognitive domain. Children must know what they're good at and how that looks, sounds, and feels. They must then embrace that trait and want to do good things. Then they can use their superpowers to blast off. When children feel good about their role as a helper, they'll be healthier and they will make their world a happier place. They will live life in the ethical domain because they'll be cornering the market on character in their world.

Remember the 4-H pledge: "I pledge my head to clearer thinking, my heart to greater loyalty, my hands to larger service, and my health to better living for my club, my community, my country, and my world."

When our son Jacob was in the fifth grade, this is what he had to say about actions and words in his award-winning essay:

"Actions speak louder than words." ~American proverb[30]

The saying "actions speak louder than words" means a lot to me because actions really do speak louder. It is better to do something than to just say you will. For instance, if someone said that they were going to do community service, just saying it wouldn't be as helpful as actually doing it. I've seen a lot of posters around my school that say that character is about how you ACT. In fact, the word act is actually embedded in the word character. That quote shows a lot of character.

An example of this is when I helped increase my friend's chance to win a ping-pong table in a raffle. He only had one ticket that the teacher passed out, and, since my mom donated to our fundraiser, I'd gotten one hundred and twenty tickets. I heard him say that he would really like the ping-pong table and that he was going to put his one ticket into that bucket. When I heard this, I decided to help him by putting in a couple of my tickets with his name on them. I never told him, but it felt good to help a friend. I was very

103

excited when I heard over the announcements that he had won the ping-pong table.

Another good example of this quote in action is when my mom told me that she would help me find a job so I could earn some money. Her promise didn't help me much until she actually found me a job. She gave me the responsibility of planning our family meals, clipping coupons for the ingredients we needed, and helping her shop for these items. She helped me find a way to make money, not by her words, but by her actions. And now I have enough money to buy my whole family birthday presents.

I hope that the adage "actions speak louder than words" not only means much in my life but in yours, too. It is a great thing to keep in mind next time you're tempted to just say something instead of doing something. If you use the Six Pillars of Character, they will give you the courage to take action instead of just watching or talking about it on the sidelines. My actions helped my friend and my mom's actions helped me. If everybody were to do something for someone else, the world would be a better place!

At ten years old, Jacob understood the domains of character and his reflective essay is evidence that you're never too young to be living in the ethical domain. Our children are our future and they are, without question, my superheroes.

Sources and Resources

1. "11 Principles|CEP." Character Education Partnership. 19 Jan. 2014. www.character.org/more-resources/11-principles.

2. "Quotations: Parenting." Josephson Institute of Ethics: Quotes to Inspire. 19 Jan. 2014. josephsoninstitute.org/quotes/quotations.php?q=Parenting.

3. BrainyQuote. Xplore. 19 Jan. 2014. www.brainyquote.com/quotes/quotes/h/helenkelle101340.html.

4. Medina, John. *Brain rules: 12 Principles for Surviving and Thriving at Work, Home, and School.* Seattle, WA: Pear P, 2008.

5. Bandy, Joe. "What Is Service Learning or Community Engagement?" Center for Teaching. 19 Jan. 2014. http://cft.vanderbilt.edu/teaching-guides/teaching-through-community-engagement/.

6. Fox, Dede. "The Westwood Elementary Knitters." *Highlights.* Aug. 2008: 21.

7. "Favorite Quotations~Kindness." Daily Celebrations. 19 Jan. 2014. www.dailycelebrations.com/kind.htm.

8. Andersen, Erika. "21 Quotes from Henry Ford on Business, Leadership and Life." *Forbes.* 31 May 2013. Forbes Magazine. 19 Jan. 2014. www.forbes.com/sites/erikaandersen/2013/05/31/21-quotes-from-henry-ford-on-business-leadership-and-life.

9. "Stephen R. Covey Quotes." Good Reads. 17 Jan. 2014 www.goodreads.com/author/quotes/1538.Stephen_R_Covey.

10. Tough, Paul. *How Children Succeed: Grit, Curiosity, and the Hidden Power of Character.* London: Random House Books, 2013.

11. "Chronology: The Revolutionary War." George Washington: A

National Treasure. 19 Jan. 2014. www.georgewashington.si.edu/life/chrono_war.html.

12. Wiener, Jon. "Lincoln's Slavery Tactic." *Los Angeles Times.* 02 Jan. 2013. 19 Jan. 2014. http://articles.latimes.com/2013/jan/02/opinion/la-oe-wiener-emancipation-proclamation-20130102.

13. McCain, John S. "Prisoner of War: A First-Person Account." U.S. News & World Report. 28 Jan. 2008. 19 Jan. 2014. www.usnews.com/news/articles/2008/01/28/john-mccain-prisoner-of-war-a-first-person-account.

14. "About Helen Keller." Helen Keller, Her Life & Legacy. 18 Jan. 2014. www.hki.org/about-helen-keller.

15. "Sally Ride Science." Dr. Sally Ride. 19 Jan. 2014. https://sallyridescience.com/about-us/dr-sally-ride.

16. George, Dave. "Covering Nancy Kerrigan's Attack 20 Years Ago Was the Strangest Assignment of My Career." *The Palm Beach Post.* 17 Jan. 2014. 19 Jan. 2014. www.palmbeachpost.com/news/sports/dave-george-covering-nancy-kerrigans-attack-20-yea/ncrhM.

17. "Quotations: Work." Quoteland. 19 Jan. 2014. www.quoteland.com/topic/Work-Quotes/156.

18. "Perseverance Quotes." The Quote Garden. 19 Jan. 2014. www.quotegarden.com/perseverance.html.

19. "The Golden Rule in World Religions." Teaching Values. Adapted from "The Christopher Newsletter." 19 Jan. 2014. www.teachingvalues.com/goldenrule.html.

20. "Quotation: George Bernard Shaw." The Quotations Page. 19 Jan. 2014. www.quotationspage.com/quote/38888.html.

21. Burgess, Dave. *Teach Like a PIRATE: Increase Student Engagement,*

Boost Your Creativity, and Transform Your Life as an Educator. San Diego, CA: Dave Burgess Consulting, Inc., 2012.

22. Heatherley, Joyce Landorf. *Balcony People.* Waco, TX: Word Books, 1984.

23. "D Sunshine Vitamin." Sunshine Vitamin. 19 Jan. 2014. www.sunshinevitamin.org.

24. Bliss, Rosalie M. "Dehydration Affects Mood, Not Just Motor Skills." USDA: Agricultural Research Service. 23 Nov. 2009. 19 Jan. 2014. www.ars.usda.gov/is/pr/2009/091123.htm.

25. "Official Ziglar Quotes." The Ziglar Way. 19 Jan. 2014. www.ziglar.com/quotes/zig-ziglar/people-often-say-motivation-doesnt-last.

26. "Encouragement Quotes." BrainyQuote. Xplore. 19 Jan. 2014. www.brainyquote.com/quotes/keywords/encouragement.html.

27. "Quotes by Anatole France." Good Reads. 19 Jan. 2014. www.goodreads.com/quotes/74960-nine-tenths-of-education-is-encouragement.

28. "Encouragement Quotes." BrainyQuote. Xplore. 19 Jan. 2014. www.brainyquote.com/quotes/keywords/encouragement.html.

29. Bailey, Rebecca Anne. *Conscious discipline: 7 Basic Skills for Brain Smart Classroom Management.* Oviedo, FL: Loving Guidance, 2001.

30. "Josephson Institute of Ethics." CHARACTER COUNTS!: Foundations For Life. 19 Jan. 2014. http://charactercounts.org/programs/FFL/weekly-041909_Other3Rs.html.

Barbara Gruener is a counselor and character coach at Westwood-Bales Elementary, a National School of Character. She grew up on a family dairy farm in Wisconsin and credits life on the farm with helping build her strength of character and work ethic during her formative years. Though she'll tell you that she informally started teaching when she was in kindergarten, Barbara has worked as a teacher and counselor with students across all grades, pre-K through twelfth, for thirty years. During that time, Barbara has always used fun as her invitation to engage, create, discover, learn, and grow with her students. She feels blessed to be able to connect with kids, be a part of their stories, and help them reach their greatest potential. Her boundless energy and passionate enthusiasm have taken her from San Francisco to New Jersey and Wisconsin to Puerto Rico, sharing her message about the importance of shaping hearts and minds for the future with kindness, respect, and care. When she's not working, Barbara likes to knit, bake, read, write, and take long walks. She lives in Friendswood, Texas, with her husband, John, and their three children. Please visit Barbara at www.corneroncharacter.com.

More Praise for *What's Under Your Cape?*

"As a comprehensive, user-friendly resource that dedicated and hard-working educators will turn to time and again, this guide delivers refreshing, easily implemented, and highly effective strategies to connect with kids and capture their hearts. The use of many children's literature titles, along with question and extension suggestions, will allow practical alignment into a standards-based curriculum. *What's Under Your Cape?* is a must-have for any caring educator looking to spark character education within an authentic, fun, engaging, and practical framework!"
~Lisa Steele, Elementary School Counselor, Newport News, VA

"This book is a must-have resource for any counselor or teacher looking to infuse character into their school. Barbara connects tangible behaviors with abstract words like 'respect,' 'responsibility,' and 'empathy.' While we were able to visit her school and implement many of her ideas in our journey to becoming a National School of Character, I wish this book had been available years ago. This collection of stories and strategies is a booster shot of character and enthusiasm every educator needs!"
~Jennifer McCaffrey, Counselor at North Pointe Elementary, 2013 National School of Character, Houston, TX

"Powerful and empowering, this book simultaneously ignites inspiration, encourages by example, and wraps us in a warm hug. It's the perfect prescription for healing our world, one kindness at a time."
~Jodi Moore, Author of *When a Dragon Moves In* and *Good News Nelson*

"Barbara Gruener's book is a wonderful character education resource for elementary educators. It is filled with ideas, activities, and suggested children's literature that teachers can use as they help to instill good character into the hearts of their boys and girls. Just think what our future world would be if all of today's children grew up to become positive character superheroes—what a beautiful world that would be!" ~Pam Morgan, Retired Elementary Principal, Executive Director of Character@HEART, Montgomery, AL

"Barbara has been instrumental in 'flooding our world with character' and has provided us with not only inspiration but tools with which to grow a community of caring, compassionate citizens who feel empowered to be a positive voice for change. North Pointe Elementary has been significantly impacted for the better due to Barbara's positive energy and passion for character. This book encompasses that energy and is a must-read!" ~Kelly Mooney, Principal, North Pointe Elementary, 2013 National School of Character, Houston, TX

"This is a practical and inspirational account of how to infuse character into the fabric of every classroom and school. Parents can also see how they can expand their role as their children's primary character educators. This is a book that delivers on its promise of showing how character is impacted by thinking, feeling, and doing." ~Ron Axelrod, Retired Teacher and International Baccalaureate Coordinator, Former Staff Development Coordinator, Community of Caring CEP National Schools of Character Site Visitor

"Barbara has written a practical, well-organized, and easy-to-read guide on teaching important character traits to children. Teachers will appreciate the incorporation of hands-on activities, songs, projects, and other fun ideas for making abstract character trait concepts more concrete and helping kids recognize the importance of good character." ~Angela Watson, Owner and Founder of Due Season Press and Educational Services, Author of "The Cornerstone for Teachers" blog

"Barbara is a gifted and authentic writer! Her love and passion for teaching and building a climate of character jumps out in each chapter through her personal life stories and creative, character-building activities. Barbara's commitment to empower young lives through character development makes her, indeed, a superhero!" ~Dr. Jodi Duron, Superintendent of Schools, Elgin, TX

★ Notes ★

★ Notes ★

★ Notes ★

★ Notes ★

★ Notes ★

★ Notes ★

★ Notes ★